THE KING OF KINGS AND I

Travels with God in Thailand

Kim Louise Clarke

THE KING OF KINGS AND I
Copyright © 2019 by Kim Louise Clarke

All rights reserved. Neither this publication nor any part of this publication may be reproduced or transmitted in any form or by any means, electronic or mechanical, including photocopying, recording or any information storage and retrieval system, without permission in writing from the author.

Scripture taken from the New International Version (NIV) Holy Bible, New International Version®, NIV® Copyright ©1973, 1978, 1984, 2011 by Biblica, Inc.® Used by permission. All rights reserved worldwide.

Print ISBN: 978-1-988983-07-3
Ebook ISBN: 978-1-988983-06-6

Cover painting by Marquita Poulson
Interior photos by Kim Louise Clarke
Cover and interior design by Colleen McCubbin

Siretona Creative
Calgary, Alberta, Canada
www.siretona.com

Cataloguing in Publication may be obtained through Library and Archives Canada

Dedication

To Ian,
so thankful God's path
led me to you

Contents

Map of Thailand		7
ACKNOWLEDGEMENTS		9

CHANGE
1.	Rocky Landscape	12
2.	Searching Out a Matter	16
3.	An OK Direction	19
4.	We Three Kings	23
5.	I Spy	27

TRAVEL
6.	Letters & Landfills	32
7.	Plotting	35
8.	One Night in Bangkok	40
9.	Advice Taken	44
10	My Gift to Use	49

BEGIN
11.	Seashells by the Seashore	54
12.	Painful Blessings	59
13.	The Fear Chapter	64
14.	Flowers	68
15.	Shake it Off	71

OBSERVE
16.	Offerings	76
17.	Enlightened	81
18.	Free Indeed	84
19.	Marketplace Poverty	87

STRUGGLE
20.	Appearances	92
21.	Time Well Spent	96
22.	Somewhere Else	100
23.	Travelling Sounds	104

CONTRIBUTE
24.	What Not to Wear	108
25.	Building Bridges	111
26.	A Fantastic Arrangement	115
27.	Satisfaction	119

RETURN
28.	Wallet Woes	124
29.	The Box	128
30.	Honesty	132
31.	Walk in Wisdom	135

NOTES   140

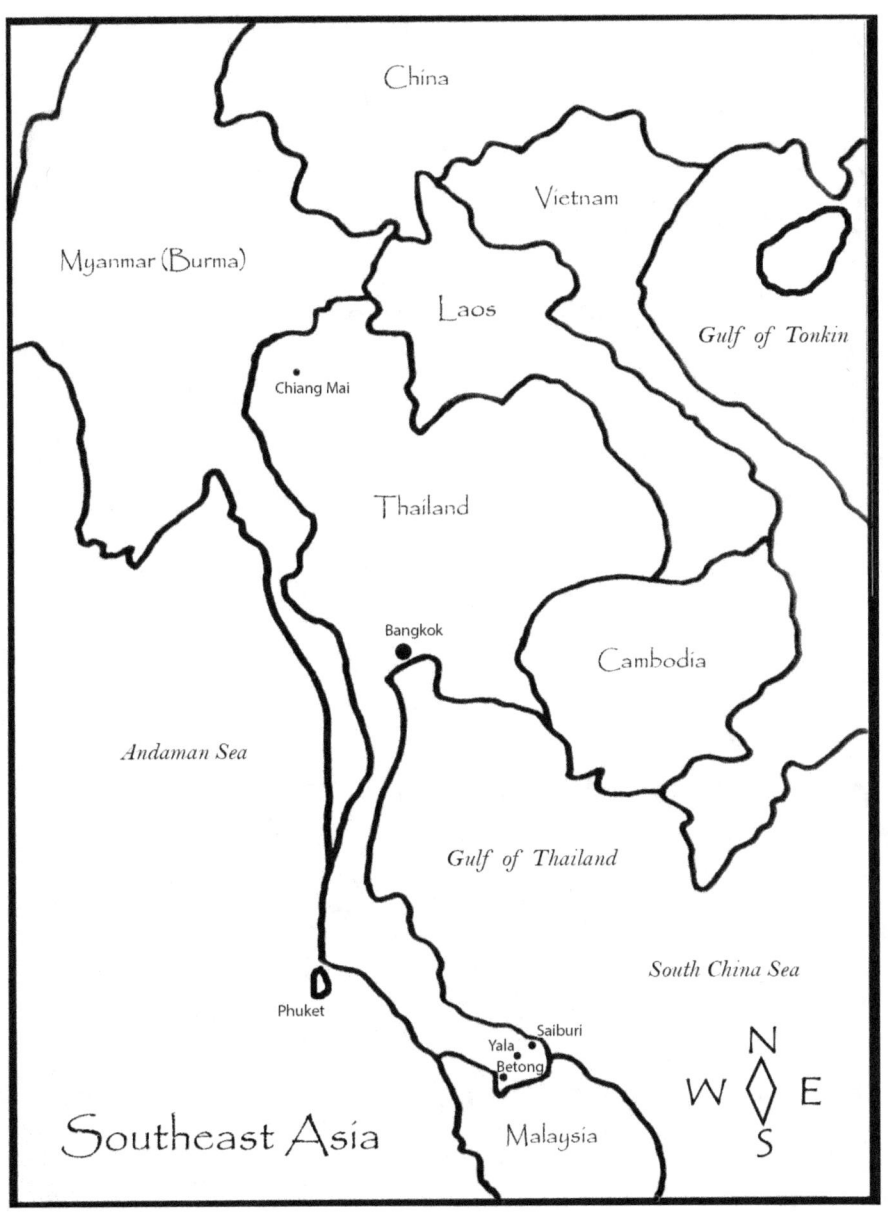

Acknowledgements

After becoming frustrated from working on a chapter, I announced to my husband "My writing is not good." He didn't refute my comment. Instead he said, "Well, then make it good." He believed that such a thing was possible and so I persisted until I liked what I wrote. I thank him for his encouragement, advice, editing, and his never tiring of my random questions.

I am thankful to my children, Hannah and Philip, for encouraging me to keep going, sharing their opinions, and being so willing to listen when I would yet again talk about writing. I also appreciate my three stepsons Jeremy, Jamie, and Leigh for their interest in my work and their encouragement. My sister Marquita, the artist behind the book cover, has offered her incredible talent as well as her support and enthusiasm, and I cannot thank her enough.

Thanks goes out to my supportive church family at Crescent Heights Baptist. I appreciate Carolyn and David for being there at the start of my Christian walk so many years ago.

Prairie Bible Institute (Prairie College) has been, and continues to be, an exceptional place to study and I am so glad God led me there. I also appreciate OMF International and their ongoing dedication to God's work in Southeast Asia. Specifically I am grateful to Robert Erion for sharing his extensive mission knowledge with me. I am thankful to both him and Rev. Judy Shierman for reading my manuscript and responding with such gracious comments.

I want to thank Carolyn at FineTune Editing for her excellent work, and also thank Colleen at Siretona Creative for her guidance and expertise in the publication process.

Hills and rice fields of south Thailand

CHANGE

Nothing happens until something moves.
                    Albert Einstein

Do not ask God to guide your footsteps if you're not willing to move your feet.
                    Sean Patrick Flanery

Chapter 1
Rocky Landscape

Can food actually mitigate bad news? I must have thought so when I drifted into an empty restaurant and ordered a steak dinner well before the noon hour. This would not be my last meal, but possibly my last expensive restaurant meal for a long time.

The restaurant should have been full of like-minded people because I was not the only one in town who had suddenly lost a job. Unemployment hit thousands of people not just in Calgary but also throughout the province. In a way it was hardly surprising, since this was Alberta, land of oil and gas, where the boom and bust economy continually cycles—except this time the cycle's downward course hit me directly. This was 1980 when the provincial economy crashed hard all the way to bust.

I was twenty-one when my administrative assistant position vanished. The independent geologist I worked for knew that he and his wife would no longer be receiving contracts from the big oil companies and no longer heading up north to the rigs. There would be no need for me to type reports about argillaceous sandstone with shale partings, grey limestone, some fluorescence, and a little porosity. Not only would I never type the hundreds of pages with all those words again, but there would also be no more lunches in trendy restaurants each time they returned from their weeks up north.

For almost two years, I had managed the office, taking care of the geological reports, files, invoices, accounts, and banking. What a great job it had been, with wonderful people. One summer, they had even paid my expenses for geology courses at the University of Alberta in Edmonton. In my time with them, they had given me so much, but one morning they had to take it all away. Businesses were crumbling around the province. The landscape was changing for many people.

So that autumn day, I left the office on Fourth Street looking for a restaurant. My day was not supposed to be like this, with a meal in front of me instead of a typewriter. I slathered butter on my baked potato, believing that in such times, there can be no such thing as too much. I cut into my thick slab of rich beef.

In the quiet atmosphere, questions milled about in my mind. *What would I do for the rest of the day? What would I do for the rest of my life?*

The recession cut a huge swath through the economy and provoked streams of similar questions from almost everyone, rural or urban, it didn't matter. *How long will this downturn last? How long will my savings pay for food and rent? How am I going to survive?*

Perhaps the most important question to ask was, "Where had I been putting my confidence?" If it had been in the economy, then indeed, I was in trouble, like realizing the tower of solid stone I had been leaning against for several years was merely a stack of empty cardboard boxes. A misplaced confidence.

The King of Kings

"On what are you basing this confidence of yours?" (2 Kings 18:19b). This was a great question, asked by one who turned out to be an overconfident king in the Old Testament. Deep into Judean territory, southwest of Jerusalem, Assyrian King Sennacherib stood poised to take over the rest of what we now know as the Middle East. He had conquered the other nations and now sought to undermine the confidence of the people of God. He challenged the Israelites to consider the changes their king had made to their landscape. How could King Hezekiah have done such abominable things, like ridding the land of the idols and altars of the gods? Hezekiah had been thorough, doing what he could to turn the people's hearts back to worshipping the one true God. He changed the landscape. "He removed the high places, smashed the sacred stones and cut down the Asherah poles" (2 Kings 18:4a).

Sennacherib was incapable of understanding. He could only see that Israel had become utterly barren—godless. He had come to believe that Israel now had nothing to rely on that superseded his own great powers. In attempting to take full advantage of Israel's apparent disarray, Sennacherib asked the wrong and ultimately fatal question. "This is what the great king, the king of Assyria, says: On what are you basing this confidence of yours? . . . If you say to me, 'We are depending on the Lord our God'—isn't he the one whose high places and altars Hezekiah removed?" (2 Kings 18:19, 22a).

King Hezekiah stood his ground, keeping his confidence in a King higher and more powerful than either himself or Sennacherib. "Lord, the God of Israel, enthroned between the cherubim, you alone are God over all the kingdoms of the earth . . . It is true, Lord, that the Assyrian kings have laid waste these nations and their lands. . . . Now, Lord our God, deliver us from his hand, so that all the kingdoms of the earth may know that you alone, Lord, are God" (2 Kings 19:15, 17, 19).

Hezekiah's prayer spelled doom for the Assyrians without Israel raising a hand. "That night the angel of the Lord went out and put to death a hundred and eighty-five thousand in the Assyrian camp" (2 Kings 19:35a). King Sennacherib returned home humiliated, later to be killed by his own sons.

And I

Where does our confidence lie when unwelcomed changes disrupt our lives—when the life we built suddenly topples? To what or to whom do we reach out? What or who do we believe can help us keep standing and not be crushed by the falling debris?

There I was, three millennia later, in 1980, in a life interrupted by an unwelcome change, but a life that possessed a faith in God. God was someone to hang onto. Someone solid to lean against amid the swirling turmoil.

I hadn't known God for long, only a year, and what I did know of Him still felt like a mere introduction. From attending church, I had become familiar with a number of powerful scriptural words describing Him. But now, in relation to the living out of my life, I needed to know Him to be who He says He is, and to do what He says He will do. *How will God, the King of kings, reign in my life? How will He direct me and provide for me? How confident am I that He even cares about me—just one of many scared and unemployed young adults?* I believed God was real, and that belief drove me to want to know Him better.

The King of Kings and I

If He is all He says He is, then what an astounding Person to know.

I understood that by studying the Scriptures a person could get to know God better. Having not been raised in a Christian home, I was off to a slow start. I entertained thoughts about studying the Bible and prayed about my life's direction within this economic chaos. What became clear to me was that I still needed to pay for food and rent, and my savings would not last long. As bad as it was, the economy did not shut down totally. A secretarial job in the geology department of an oil and gas company opened up. I returned to the world of geology, but now with thoughts about attending Bible college.

Eventually I made the decision. I didn't like quitting a job after only eight months, but I knew in such economic times, they would have no difficulty replacing me.

I had prayerfully considered several colleges. The internationally well-known Prairie Bible Institute, now known as Prairie College, was situated in Three Hills, a small town about one hundred and thirty kilometres driving distance northeast of Calgary. My parents happened to live in another small town between Calgary and Three Hills. Prairie seemed a logical choice.

I quit my job and applied for a four-year program. This would mean big changes. Born in Calgary, I loved city life, especially living by myself in my downtown apartment. And I loved my home church where they had welcomed me when I stepped into the building seeking a faith community where I could belong.

I packed everything I owned and moved out of my apartment, storing my furniture in my parents' basement. I left the downtown high rises and settled, for a time, out on the open prairie. There, I would get to know God, whom King Hezekiah described as being "God over all the kingdoms of the earth" (2 Kings 19:15b). This was the King I was putting my confidence in.

Chapter 2
Searching Out a Matter

In the early 1900s John Fergus Kirk, then seventeen years old, ventured west from Ontario. He married, bought a farm near Three Hills, Alberta, and began a Sunday school class. The Sunday school was not enough. His desire to have the Bible taught continued to grow. He offered his farm to God and sought after a Bible teacher. Leslie Ernest (L.E.) Maxwell arrived from Kansas in September 1922 to help Kirk establish a new school, and they started a Bible class with eight students.

The school grew steadily, becoming the Prairie Bible Institute. By the time I arrived in 1981, over 650 students attended the college. Including the high school, the student body added up to a little over 900.

During my freshman year, Prairie celebrated its 60th year as a Bible Institute. It was a time when Prairie was slowly undergoing rule and regulation changes. When I showed the list of rules to my mom, a WWII veteran, she remarked on how it reminded her of her army days. I thought that if she endured four years of army life for king and country, surely I could handle four years of college for the King of kings and His kingdom.

Unlike the army, we did not have to wear uniforms. We could wear our own clothes, but under certain restrictions that drastically reduced my wardrobe. Many of my tops had sleeves that were too short and failed to reach an adequate length between the shoulder and elbow. Skirts or dresses, few of which I owned, had to be worn on campus at all times. Jeans and slacks could only be worn in the dorm. For most meals, boys ate on one side of the cafeteria and girls on the other. The same division applied to the regular chapel meetings in the tabernacle.

I was not used to rules. Being home before dark had been the

The King of Kings and I

main rule in my home as I grew up. My first few weeks on campus had me feeling nervous and lost. But I had come to Prairie to study God's word and once I settled in, I found that the rules and regulations were not difficult to follow. I even found that some of the rules could be bent, if not broken. By talking with the women's dean and having sufficient reason, I could get an extra weekend off campus if I had used up my allotted three for the semester. I also reminded myself that Prairie was in the midst of change. The beginning of each new school year in September brought changes and a new freedom as Prairie sought to relax its regulations. The administration knew the direction they wanted the school to go, and with prayer, they went ahead.

Living there soon became a comfortable routine. Three meals a day in the cafeteria never failed to satisfy. Despite not needing to concern myself with groceries, food prep, or doing dishes, I still had work to do. Every student was offered a paid position, a way of pitching in to help run the school. Some students worked in the cafeteria, some in the infirmary, and some were teachers' aides. Because of my experience and maturity, being twenty-two while most freshmen were a mere eighteen, I anticipated my employment being in an office, helping out in administration. I was sure I would be behind a typewriter. I was wrong and found myself behind a large broom sweeping the high school floors. I learned a lesson in humility and found a welcomed peacefulness walking up and down the aisles of empty desks.

I spent most of my time immersing myself in Bible study—the reason why I came in the first place. The Old Testament grew more and more fascinating. I discovered that many Old Testament prophecies had been fulfilled in the New Testament, with many yet to be fulfilled. For many students this was old news, something they had probably known since kindergarten. But for me this new knowledge was thrilling. I saw the Old and New Testaments working together to reveal the same story—the story of Jesus Christ.

The King of Kings

I was doing what King Solomon described as "searching out a matter." He wrote in Proverbs 25:2, "It is the glory of God to conceal a matter; to search out a matter is the glory of kings." Not that I was a king or queen, but because I followed Christ, I belonged to His kingdom. That gave me all the credentials I needed to search out God's concealed matters.

A matter may be concealed by God, but that does not mean it necessarily has to remain that way. If kings are supposed to search out matters that God has kept secret, then it must be possible for us to do likewise. God invites us to seek Him and when we do we can uncover glorious truths about Him. The 'glory' for both God and king is the Hebrew word *kâbôd*, which carries the idea of 'weight,' in the sense that the glory to be sought is weighted with splendour. When we seek to uncover and understand, we will find copious spiritual truths that abound in glory. "'You will seek me and find me when you seek me with all your heart. I will be found by you,' declares the Lord" (Jeremiah 29:13-14a).

King Hezekiah set an example of someone who searched the Scriptures. He became well aware of the ancient writings of King Solomon, who ruled two and a half centuries before him. And in studying God's written word, King Hezekiah grasped its importance and played a huge role in restoring Scripture to his people. In fact, the 25th Proverb begins with: "These are more proverbs of Solomon, compiled by the men of Hezekiah king of Judah" (Proverbs 25:1).

Under Hezekiah's rule, people's lives changed because the word of the Lord was being lived out. From one king (Solomon) to another king (Hezekiah) the word of God was written, read, searched out, treasured, compiled, and acted upon.

And I

I wanted to do the same as King Hezekiah. I wanted to invest my time searching out the spiritual matters of God and Prairie proved to be a perfect place to do this. Jesus says a lot about the importance for believers to invest in His Kingdom. This was the kingdom I belonged to.

"The kingdom of heaven is like a merchant looking for fine pearls. When he found one of great value, he went away and sold everything he had and bought it" (Matthew 13:45-46).

Chapter 3
An OK Direction

It didn't take long for me to discover that the student body could be divided into three unofficial groups. It was hardly surprising at Prairie, a mission-minded school with the motto "Know Christ and Make Him Known," that one large group consisted of MKs—missionary kids. Many of their parents had attended Prairie, had become missionaries, and now had their own adult children enrolled there. I found the life of an MK as foreign to me as if they had lived on the moon. They had grown up in Bolivia, or South Africa, or Indonesia, or some such country. Some of them would have left home at six to attend a distant missionary school, being away from home for months at a time. Every fourth year being a furlough year, their entire family would pack up everything and fly off to spend it in a strange country called Canada or the United States.

The PKs were the preachers' kids, raised in Christian homes, and attending church once or perhaps twice every Sunday. Some had experienced several moves as their father relocated from one church to another, from city to city, province to province, or even country to country. Their lives, too, were foreign to me.

The last category included all the other students, including me—the OKs or the ordinary kids. It didn't matter if you grew up in a Christian home or a secular home. Your life ran along ordinary and stationary lines, where uprooting was not the norm. Almost all of my life had been in Calgary, and I had little experience in uprooting from the familiar and the comfortable. I had travelled for vacations, but Calgary had always been home.

My first two years of listening to fascinating missionary

speakers, as well as getting to know some MKs, had me considering spending one of my summers between school terms doing mission work. Many students, whether MKs, PKs, or OKs, did summer missions.

I had been attending my home church for two years before entering Prairie and the two friends I first met at church were missionaries—great people who influenced my life profoundly. Carolyn worked with a children's mission within the city. She taught me as I helped out in our church's Sunday school. She showed me ways to teach Bible lessons creatively, to convey the meaning clearly, and in a way that made it fun for the children. By her dedication she showed me how precious children were to Christ and convinced me that we needed to see them the same way. And so, when it came to choosing a degree program, the Bachelor of Religious Education seemed a practical and fitting program for me to choose.

The other person at church who influenced my life was David, who also worked in children's ministry. He had a passion for reaching out to those who didn't know Christ. This led him to look into overseas mission work. While I was at Prairie, he had been accepted to work in South Thailand serving with Overseas Missionary Fellowship (now known as OMF International). It seemed a natural fit for me to choose Missions as the minor in my degree program.

Unlike most students at Prairie, I had extra optional classes to fill because I simply could not sing well. After the requisite but embarrassing audition, thankfully only in front of the music teacher, I was informed that I need not be part of the student choir. About ten other non-singing students shared my 'condition' and we were required to choose other courses to make up the choir credits that were impossible for us to earn. Thankfully, Prairie did not lack in mission courses to choose from.

I learned about world religions and church history. I wrote essays about missions in the local church. But in reading missionary biographies, I gravitated to missionaries of the 1800's. The books gave me some understanding of missionaries' cultural and spiritual struggles but they could not give me that personal experience. The printed pages failed to envelop me in drenching humidity, scorching heat, or thick green jungle, as was common for the missionaries I read about. Having knowledge about something isn't the same as having experience.

Even though two more years of college lay ahead, there were moments when I wondered what I would do with my life afterward. Perhaps missions might play a part, and a summer in a faraway country with heat, humidity, and jungle would help me decide if that was a vocation to explore after graduation. Despite not having clarity about my goal in life, I wanted experience to go along with my head knowledge. As Oliver Wendell Holmes Jr. put it, "A mind that is stretched by a new experience can never go back to its old dimensions."

Many excellent organizations like Overseas Missionary Fellowship (OMF) were represented at Prairie's annual mission conferences. OMF offered a varied summer program for students in several Southeast Asian countries. I didn't have a burden for any particular people group or country, but I considered what I'd do and sensed that a short-term mission anywhere was a promising idea.

The King of Kings

I believed that the Lord wanted me to put into practice what I was learning. "Do not merely listen to the word, and so deceive yourselves. Do what it says" (James 1:22).

Be a doer of the word. The root word for 'do,' *pŏiētēs* in Greek, contains the idea of performing. It also means poet. A doer of the word listens to God's words, and then does something with them. It's as if we are to take God's words and perform them, live them out, as a poet would take words and craft them into a meaningful and beautiful form of art. The words "Go and make disciples of all nations" (Matthew 28:19a) involve commitment and action and that is what I wanted—to do and act upon God's words.

Jesus knew how to teach His disciples, reinforcing their knowledge with experience. The disciples followed Christ from town to town, witnessed miracles, listened to teachings, and were given the privilege of His exclusive insights into them.

But Jesus knew He would be leaving them soon and so He prepared them for a life of walking by faith. The disciples would follow a teacher they could no longer see but would know by the Holy Spirit. They would become the visible body of Christ to the world.

Jesus prepared the disciples by sending them on a mission without Him. That experience would add to their knowledge. Jesus sent the twelve disciples out two by two (Mark 6:6-12), and then sent out another group of seventy-two, also by twos. Jesus told the disciples up front that while it would not be easy, it was of eternal importance because it had to do with the kingdom of God. He told them, "Go! I am sending you out like lambs among wolves. . . . When you enter a town and are welcomed, eat what is offered to you. Heal the sick who are there and tell them, 'The kingdom of God has come near to you'" (Luke 10:3, 8-9).

Jesus' followers returned from a memorable mission. The seventy-two joyfully came back to Him and said, "Lord, even the demons submit to us in your name" (Luke 10:17).

And I

God wants to shape us to be effective in the world. Like the disciples and early church, we are members of the body of Christ needing to move in the world to let people know of His kingdom.

I wanted to add a new chapter to my education, an experience chapter about being 'sent out.' I wanted to take the words I had been studying and perform them—to produce His poetry with them. Midway through my sophomore year, I applied to OMF for a summer mission in Thailand. I was accepted and ploughed through the paperwork. I would be a SPOT (Summer Program of Overseas Training) worker. The road to Thailand seemed clear, an OK direction for an OK.

CHAPTER 4

We Three Kings

One concern loomed over my preparations for my trip to Thailand—money. How could I do this financially? Employment to pay my tuition occupied my summer months between school years. Now I would miss two of those summer months, while needing an extra $3,000 for an overseas trip.

I knew the encouraging phrases in Psalm 50: "for every animal of the forest is mine, and the cattle on a thousand hills" (verse 10) and "the world is mine, and all that is in it" (verse 12b). I knew that God owned everything, and that I could ask Him for whatever I needed, and He could easily supply my need out of His rich bounty.

But I had never asked God for money before. How would He do it? He could flutter dollar bills down from the sky, but I didn't think He would. It seemed to me that God usually works through the natural order of things and through established paths, such as: you work and then you get paid. It also seemed to me that God often had us playing a part in answering our own prayers, while at the same time remaining dependent upon Him.

It made sense that I should look for a job at the end of April despite only being able to work until mid-June. As my sophomore year ended, I looked into secretarial work in Calgary. An agency accepted me in a secretary/receptionist role and I became available as a 'temp' for companies needing someone to fill in for an employee away on vacation or sick leave. This type of employment can be sporadic, but I was provided with consistent work up to my departure date.

Financial support also came from my home church, my family, and my friends, who gave toward my trip. My responsibility was to humbly accept these sacrificial gifts and to be accountable for each cent. Meanwhile my senior year's tuition became something I would need to trust God for in the future. For the moment it needed to be put aside. I trusted God would also help me with that when the time came.

James Hudson Taylor (1832-1905) founded the mission I signed up with. It began as the China Inland Mission (CIM). Hudson Taylor wanted to venture inland, where the residing throngs of rural people needed to know Jesus Christ. He loved and respected the Chinese people. He wanted Chinese Christians to be the leaders in their churches and the church buildings to be designed in the Chinese architectural style. In 1900 a Chinese group called the "Boxers" wanted to rid China of all foreigners. During this time of persecution, hundreds of Christians, both foreign and Chinese, were killed. CIM remained in China but felt the need to finally withdraw in 1950 when tensions increased. Once again, the presence of foreigners in China had become increasingly unwelcome, making things especially difficult for the Chinese Christians.

CIM took its head office to Singapore and changed its name to OMF and the missionaries began their work in neighbouring Asian countries. One of Hudson Taylor's most famous quotes was never too far from my thoughts as I prepared for serving with OMF: "God's work done in God's way will never lack God's supply."

The King of Kings

I saw God providing the supply I needed. He would not fail me, just as He never failed the Israelites I was studying. God's plan for the Israelites who were captive in Babylon included returning to Jerusalem, rebuilding the temple that lay in ruins, and once again offering sacrifices. How would that come about? No doubt it would be in answer to the prayers of God's people, and it would involve their faith, their courage, and their labour.

Despite the historically confusing reigns and even the names of the kings of Persia, we can see how God worked through three kings in particular to bring about the restoration of His temple. Through them God would provide all the supplies—gold, or silver, or whatever was needed.

The King of Kings and I

King number one was King Cyrus who said: "The Lord, the God of heaven, has given me all the kingdoms of the earth and he has appointed me to build a temple for him at Jerusalem in Judah. . . . And in any locality where survivors may now be living, the people are to provide them with silver and gold" (Ezra 1:2, 4a).

Opposition had the temple rebuilding come to a stop. But then, under the reign of king number two, King Darius, the rebuilding continued. Darius himself decreed: "Do not interfere with the work on this temple of God. . . . Their expenses are to be fully paid out of the royal treasury" (Ezra 6:7a, 8b).

After the completion of the temple restoration, God worked through king number three, King Artaxerxes: "Moreover, you are to take with you the silver and gold that the king and his advisers have freely given to the God of Israel . . . With this money be sure to buy bulls, rams . . . and sacrifice them on the altar of the temple of your God." (Ezra 7:15, 17).

God provided through these three Persian kings, so that once again His people could worship Him in His temple.

There is another scriptural example where God provided for His people, through specific individuals. We sing "We Three Kings" at Christmas, although we don't know if there were three, and they probably were not kings but 'magi,' traditionally called 'wise men,' perhaps even astrologers. "On coming to the house, they saw the child with his mother Mary, and they bowed down and worshiped him. Then they opened their treasures and presented him with gifts of gold, frankincense and myrrh" (Matthew 2:11).

They presented Jesus with three significant gifts. After the Magi's visit, Mary, Joseph, and the infant Jesus fled to Egypt for a time. The gifts from the Magi could very well have been the needed resources that helped them manage their stay in Egypt, until they could return to their family home and where Joseph could return to work as a carpenter.

And I

I grew up having a brother whom I rarely saw. If he wasn't up north on an oil rig, or taking courses in Texas, or working in Yemen, or exploring the Arctic, he was somewhere else in the world and no one in the family knew where. He happened to be at my parent's house one day when I was also there, just a short while before my mission trip. The two of us ventured to the local mall. He bought me a pop and when he opened his wallet to pay, he also pulled out a bill, and told me it was for my trip to Thailand. It was a red fifty-dollar bill with a 'King' on it—Prime Minister William Lyon Mackenzie King.

In His supplying my financial needs, God's hand moved through the usual and enough of the unusual for me to sense His gentle hand moving to answer my prayers. By the time I left for the airport, I had $3,000 for my trip, and I could return knowing that my upcoming year's tuition was paid for.

The way might look impossible. How would the temple be rebuilt? How would Mary and Joseph manage? How would things come together for my trip? We need not worry. God always has a king or two at His disposal. He always provides what we need to do His will.

Chapter 5
I Spy

OMF sent me their information about Thailand, providing facts about the population, politics, customs, and sports. It gave me a full breakdown of the country by occupations, religions, and people groups.

I also received their photocopied map of South Thailand. It was not to scale, but its hand-drawn symbols and typewritten labels provided interesting information. Dots and squares of varying sizes represented towns, small district centres, and even markets along roadsides. The map indicated the areas where missionaries worked and where churches had been established. Sketches of grouped palm trees illustrated coconut crops, and another clump of trees represented rubber tree plantations. The geography included the hilly areas, rice fields, waterfalls, and the railroad tracks running through the south right into the bordering country of Malaysia.

Twice in the hilly areas near the rubber trees, I noticed indications of 'gorilla activity.' But on closer examination I found that I was mistaken. Looking more carefully at the spelling, I realized that the map indicated 'guerilla activity' of the Communist kind. I thought that coming face to face with either a gorilla or guerilla would be terrifying. Studying the map further, I noticed that one of the towns I would be staying in showed as a little dot off the side of a road. The road curved between the words, 'guerilla' and 'activity.' I suddenly felt that I had too much information.

What should I do with it? The first thing I did was to hide the map from my parents since I didn't want them to worry. I could do enough worrying for all of us. I wondered about my short-term mission trip. *How adventurous was this going to be? Should I even go?*

What do we do when we have too much information? When it takes us from excitement to worry? When we begin to entertain alternative plans from what we thought was God's program to begin with, because of fear.

Sometimes we gather so much information trying to cover all possible scenarios of what could go wrong—as if we have to be God—and depend on ourselves to deal with the problems. We research places to death, so that upon arrival, we know more facts about the place than the locals do. But the local people will always know their place in a way we don't. And God knows the places where He sends us even better. Where is the balance between responsible planning and trusting God?

The King of Kings

Acquiring information about a country we plan to visit is not a bad thing to do. Having current information to prepare ourselves is smart. In the days of the Old Testament, people also gathered information about countries they were about to enter, not as missionaries or tourists, but as conquerors in preparation for their invasion. To retrieve information, armies often sent out spies.

Under God's direction, the sending out of spies brought encouragement. God directed Gideon to attack the Midianites. Before the attack God said to Gideon, "If you are afraid to attack, go down to the camp with your servant Purah and listen to what they are saying. Afterward, you will be encouraged to attack the camp" (Judges 7:10-11a). Good comes out of the information God provides for us.

But when I read the passage about Israel, I wondered if God intended the Israelites to spy out the land of Canaan in the first place or simply go and take possession of it. We read Moses's words: "Then all of you came to me and said, 'Let us send men ahead to spy out the land for us and bring back a report about the route we are to take and the towns we will come to.' The idea seemed good to me; so I selected twelve of you, one man from each tribe" (Deuteronomy 1:22-23). Perhaps it was because of the Israelite's insistence to spy out the land that the Lord then told Moses

The King of Kings and I

to send out spies (Numbers 13:1-2).

The spies returned with a good news-bad news report. "It is a good land that the Lord our God is giving us" (Deuteronomy 1:25b).

But the bad news describing the strong Canaanites within their tall city walls terrified the people. The efforts of the spies, Joshua and Caleb, to encourage the people to trust God went ignored. A rebellion broke out, causing that generation to spend the next forty years in the wilderness. This eventually allowed the next generation to stand at the doorway to the Promised Land.

Standing at the doorway with them were Joshua and Caleb, the only spies who remained alive to return to the land with this next generation. As they camped ready to enter the Promised Land, Joshua, now the leader, secretly sent out two spies. He must have believed that two good spies were sufficient! The spies returned saying: "The Lord has surely given the whole land into our hands; all the people are melting in fear because of us" (Joshua 2:24).

It would seem that the sending out of these two spies was God's direction. So much good came out of it. Not only was Joshua, the new leader, encouraged, but the woman Rahab and her family were spared. "So the king of Jericho sent this message to Rahab: 'Bring out the men who came to you and entered your house, because they have come to spy out the whole land'" (Joshua 2:3). Because Rahab feared the God of Israel more than the king of Jericho, she helped the spies escape. When the Israelites attacked the city, she and her family were spared and joined the Israelites. Rahab would become part of the lineage of Jesus Christ, the coming Messiah (Matthew 1:5).

Joshua knew how tall the walls were around the cities and how tall the people were. He had seen it all forty years before. He knew all about the bad news, but he focused on the good. Joshua didn't have to know all the details, nor understand everything. He knew enough. God was giving the Israelites this land.

And I

I don't remember details about what I did to overcome my concerns about the guerillas. I may have spoken to OMF reps or visiting missionaries to Prairie. I do remember viewing Thailand as one of the most stable countries in Southeast Asia. It was a country with enough stability that many families serving in various missions, including OMF, lived and ministered there. The fact that OMF sent summer students there also provided evidence that Thailand was stable. Although initially concerned, I remember that the cloud of worry did not hang over my head as I prepared for my trip. I found another Hudson Taylor quote encouraging: "All our difficulties are only platforms for the manifestations of His grace, power and love."

I continued with my preparations, sending my passport to the Royal Thai Consulate in Toronto to be stamped and dated for a tourist visa. The Certificate of Vaccination booklet issued by Health and Welfare Canada accumulated checkmarks and initials as I received the necessary needle jabs for typhoid, polio, cholera, and tetanus. I had malaria pills ready for the time overseas, as well as the necessary supply to follow upon my return.

I kept going forward with growing excitement, preparing to travel in the direction I believed God was pointing.

The Marketplace

TRAVEL

We travel not to escape life, but for life not to escape us.
                    Anonymous

Toto, I have a feeling we are not in Kansas anymore.
                    Dorothy
              in *The Wizard of Oz*
              by L. Frank Baum

Chapter 6
Letters & Landfills

June 16, 1983, I said goodbye to family and friends and boarded Air Canada's flight 769 at Calgary's not-yet-international airport.

Before I left, my sister gave me a dark green covered journal called Travel Happenings. At some point on that journey I began writing my travel happenings. The adventures I had yet to experience would be detailed there over the next two months, probably filling the entire journal.

I had no idea then that years after my Thai trip, my travel journal would meet its demise. A de-cluttering frenzy would overtake me. City-wide paper recycling lay decades away, so my journal would find its way to a Calgary landfill site. In a landfill, paper takes two to six weeks to decompose. I would bury my writings among bags of garbage. My stories would decompose and die.

Fortunately, the practice of handwriting and mailing letters—the kind which required walking to a mailbox—remained popular. My Mom valued every letter I sent from Thailand and threw none of them away. Later, even when she was forced to downsize, she refused to toss them in the garbage. Instead she returned my letters to me and I kept them, storing them with all the letters from friends and family that I had received in Thailand.

Letters can be like a treasure box filled with gems of encouragement. The words can strengthen us when we are stumbling around in the faraway and the unknown.

The King of Kings

The power of a personal letter should not be underestimated. God knows the value of letters and has written a compilation of letters for us. As the King of kings residing in the heavens, His words bridge the distance between heaven and earth. He has written so as to establish and maintain His relationship with us.

God began His writing using stone. He had to print a second edition of the ten commandments, since Moses smashed the first 'print run' upon the ground. It seemed God's writing wasn't off to a great start. But Moses's action expressed his righteous anger toward the Israelites' sin (Exodus 32:15-19). He treasured God's word and emphasized to the Israelites the importance of not allowing it to remain dormant. His message: Do not ignore God's letters to you. "These commandments that I give you today are to be on your hearts. Impress them on your children. Talk about them when you sit at home and when you walk along the road, when you lie down and when you get up" (Deuteronomy 6:6-7).

Using materials such as metal, wood, clay, parchment, and animal skins to capture God's words over the centuries, faithful leaders and prophets recorded God's letters to His people so that generation after generation would benefit from them. Whatever form God's words took, the ruling kings of the day had the choice to read, respect, and teach them or ignore God's message to His people.

Kings like Jehoiakim of Judah displayed an astonishing disrespect for God's written words. "Whenever Jehudi had read three or four columns of the scroll, the king cut them off with a scribe's knife and threw them into the firepot, until the entire scroll was burned in the fire. The king and all his attendants who heard all these words showed no fear" (Jeremiah 36:23-24).

Throughout time, God's written word has had mixed reviews in the broken stone, burned leather or shredded parchment. But God persisted with writing His letters. Nothing could deter Him from revealing His Word to every generation.

After the days of the Old Testament, God's word took on a glorious form to usher in the New Covenant. "The Word became flesh and made his dwelling among us" (John 1:14a). And Jesus Christ, the Living Word of God, proved indestructible. After His crucifixion, He rose from the dead and ascended to heaven. God then continued his writing through Christ's apostles who took to recording His story, so that the church today has the New Testament to accompany the Old Testament.

But God's letter writing is not done. Even with the completed Scriptures and the completion of Christ's atoning work, God's letter writing continues today. The Apostle Paul writes: "You, yourselves are our letter, written on our hearts, known and read by everybody. You show that you are a letter from Christ . . . written not with ink but with the Spirt of the Living God, not on tablets of stone but on tablets of human hearts" (2 Corinthians 3:2-3).

And I

I am a letter. People read me. And it is Christ's message that people are to read when they look at my life. So I need to ask: Do I come across like hard chiselled stone, or can people read in me Spirit-filled words offering them life and freedom?

Some people hear what we have to say and welcome us and God's message. Others would rather toss us into a landfill site where they think our message will die. Our message, like Christ will never remain dead. It is God's message to the world. Paul talks about being in chains in prison, but he reminds us that "God's word is not chained" (2 Timothy 2:9b).

Our responsibility lies in bearing accurate content with graceful delivery. "Known and read by everybody," Paul says. What an opportunity we have to be a living letter, revealing the New Covenant in Christ and allowing the Holy Spirit to reveal this new life to those who read us. And what an opportunity I had to travel across the world, as a letter to be read by everyone I met.

Chapter 7
Plotting

I like C.S. Lewis's quote about travel:

> The truest and most horrible claim made for modern transport is that it 'annihilates space'. It does. It annihilates one of the most glorious gifts we have been given. It is a vile inflation which lowers the value of distance, so that a modern boy travels a hundred miles with less sense of liberation and pilgrimage and adventure than his grandfather got from travelling ten.

I understand Lewis's observation that modern travel diminishes not only the length but also the adventure of a trip. But from my perspective, my journey in 1983 to the other side of the world, covering 10,000 miles, took a long time. Twenty hours on planes and nine hours wandering through airports waiting for connecting flights filled my journey with passing spaces of time. And because my travels included interacting at five airports in four countries, I felt the value of the distance and the sense of a great adventure.

Each airport became less and less familiar, as if preparing me for the immersion in an Eastern culture. By crossing the International Date Line, I missed living the day of June 17, 1983. But the lengthy travel days of June 16th and 18th made up for it.

In a letter to my parents I wrote about the airline food and enjoying a steak dinner—this one up in the clouds. My life circumstances had changed since that day a few years ago when I sat alone, unemployed, eating a steak. I now had direction for my life and places to go.

Kim Louise Clarke

My letters reveal imperfections. Sentences in blue ink show squashed words inserted here and there in my attempt to clarify something. Occasionally, light strokes cross out words to minimize the appearance of an error. I wish my letter writing had been better. Having enrolled in a degree program at Prairie, I was automatically enrolled in a basic English course focusing on grammar. It was a great help when writing essays and papers, but good grammar and creativity didn't seem to find their way into my letter writing.

> Mom and Dad, Everything worked out fine in San Francisco. From Calgary to S.F. I had a window seat. It was super to see all the clouds and sunset. In Honolulu I had an hour to walk around... . Well, I'm now in Hong Kong. I have eight hours to wait. I do get a free lunch though in the cafeteria. I'm watching the planes take off and land.
> Hong Kong is a mass of high rises and behind them barren mountains. There are lots of ships in the harbour. (Hope you don't mind if I keep rambling on – it keeps me busy!) I've been reading a book about George Müller. Quite good.

At sunset in San Francisco, I boarded Singapore Airlines heading west, but flying toward the eastern lands of the Orient. I was flying the farthest from home that I had ever been. On Singapore Airlines, the earthy western familiarity disappeared with the sun, and an exotic eastern excitement filled the aircraft's atmosphere.

The flight attendants on that flight bordered on perfection and their uniforms were exquisite. In researching, I discovered that French fashion designer Paul Balmain created these uniforms in 1968 and since then has had little need to update his design. The women flight attendants still wear individually tailored sarong kebaya, which are long wrap-around skirts, with matching fitted tops. The material is a lovely breathable quality cotton in a colourful batik pattern. Chief flight attendants in red, leading stewards in green, and basic flight stewards in blue all know the importance of their dress code. Their limited eye shadow palette must match their uniform, and therefore correspond to their rank. Their nail and lip colour also match. Nail length for both men and women attendants is specified. Men are not allowed beards or moustaches. There are five hair styles for women, with the bun style having specific measurements. These flight attendants are hired from nine Asian countries, and go through extensive training to become the gracious, professional hosts that are known today worldwide.

The first flight I ever took was from Calgary to Winnipeg when I was sixteen. So when an Asian flight attendant dressed in a beautiful sarong and elegant slipper-like flats offered me duck a l'orange, and afterwards, with tongs in hand, presented me with a small hot damp white towel, I knew I was not flying to Winnipeg.

However, there was something about Singapore Air's flight attendants that disturbed me. Ignoring their borderline perfection proved difficult. Never a hair out of place, perfect fingernails, and stunning uniforms. Any passenger would be heading down a troublesome path if they were to compare themselves with this perceived perfection.

Well into my flying adventure to Bangkok, I was having thoughts that I would never have entertained a mere thousand miles before. By comparing myself to the perfection of the flight attendants, I had now become Miss Drab from the boring west. My imperfections grew in proportion with my emerging insecurities. My mousy brown hair had no style. My fingernails were not elegant. The color of my clothes faded with every passing mile. I hadn't packed a lot of clothes, but I knew that none of them held such richness in colour, fabric or design. Most were 'seventies' beige or brown, and all of them were dull.

In order to deal with this sudden personal crisis I had conjured up, I started plotting. The spending money I had saved for souvenirs, I now felt must be spent on clothes. Souvenir clothes for myself. I doubted that I would have time in Bangkok to shop for clothes, but when I arrived at my first destination, Yala in the south of the country, I hoped to whip out and buy a few tops. Something in basic flight attendant colours of blue, with hints of red and orange. Something I could wear so that I wouldn't be mistaken for a tree trunk. Something to make me feel better about myself and give me a little confidence.

Kim Louise Clarke

The King of Kings

Plotting—that's what we do. Desperate thoughts tumble in one after another and we scramble to come up with a plan. From the depths of our insecurities, a threatening situation arises and we must deal with it. Thoughts of God and our spiritual mission have to be put behind, so that we are positioned at the front. There, unhindered by God and common sense, we can do something.

This happens with the trivial, but it can also develop in more serious situations, where we lose sight of God and follow through with our own plan, making a mess and paying dire consequences.

Jeroboam is a good example of a king whom God presents with an incredible opportunity. "However, as for you, I will take you, and you will rule over all that your heart desires; you will be king over Israel. If you do whatever I command you and walk in obedience to me . . . I will be with you" (1 Kings 11:37-38a).

God's announcement to Jeroboam through the prophet Ahijah came with a promise and even a sign. Ahijah tore his new cloak into twelve pieces giving Jeroboam ten pieces, representing ten tribes of Israel that he would be responsible for as king.

But Jeroboam had no confidence in God's direction. God's plan became problematic to him and so he plotted. "Jeroboam thought to himself, 'The kingdom will now likely revert to the house of David. If these people go up to offer sacrifices at the temple of the Lord in Jerusalem, they will again give their allegiance to their lord, Rehoboam king of Judah. They will kill me and return to King Rehoboam'" (1 Kings 12:26-27).

Jeroboam had so little trust that he even imagined his own death. In desperation, he decided to act on his own by setting up two golden calves so the people he ruled over would not need to go up to Jerusalem (1 Kings 12:28-30).

In the end, striving on his own to reign over the kingdom God had given him, Jeroboam could not hold on to those ten pieces of new cloth. God's message came to him, again through the prophet Ahijah: "You have done more evil than all who lived before you. You have made for yourself other gods, idols made of metal; you have aroused my anger and turned your back on me" (1 Kings 14:9).

Even in the opportunity given him by God, Jeroboam had no

faith. He worried and put together his own plan when God already had a plan. Jeroboam turned his back on God and stepped forward into disaster, taking the Israelites with him.

And I

Self-originating disasters can easily loom up when I lose sight of my initial mission and refuse to believe in God's ability to care for me. I could have chosen to read further into my George Müller book, where his words could have proven helpful: "The beginning of anxiety is the end of faith, and the beginning of true faith is the end of anxiety." Instead, I wasted a chunk of time, plotting to buy clothes. *I must have a better wardrobe. Even just a few new pieces would help. When can I shop?*

The concerns that had begun to plague me on Singapore Airlines flew away the moment I landed in Bangkok. My wardrobe worries became immaterial. I no longer cared about how I looked. Stepping out of the airport into the humidity, the noise, and busyness of the city overwhelmed me. Getting to the OMF mission house took precedence. The real mission came back into focus and I looked to God, whom I had now placed back in the centre of my mind. I sought Him for His guidance for the next part of my journey—to get across the city of Bangkok.

Chapter 8
One Night in Bangkok

Following the instructions given me by OMF, I stepped outside the Bangkok airport doors into the muggy afternoon, needing to fend off a barrage of taxi offers, tourist excursion trips, and free pamphlets. The correct airporter bus transporting passengers to various hotels arrived, and I stepped on board. After stopping at several hotels, none of them mine, I assumed that my hotel must be at the bottom of the list.

I had a window seat and took in the unobstructed views of the city. But I grew more and more uncomfortable. A large man sitting behind me kept trying to start a conversation, asking me personal questions. At each hotel stop, he attempted to find out which hotel I had booked into. I did my best to ignore him, but when it came to my stop, I stood up and panicked at his words: "Ah, looks like we are staying at the same hotel!"

I gathered my suitcase and large duffle bag and flew out of the bus doors like a shot from a cannon. I rushed through the hotel doors, landing on both feet in the lobby. My instructions were to phone the mission house, and from there someone from OMF would pick me up. In my rattled state to distance myself from the man on the bus, I did not think to proceed to the hotel reception desk. Instead I entered the hotel restaurant to my right, because it was the first thing I noticed as I hurried through the doors. Inside I asked to use their phone, relieved that the hostess understood English and obliged me.

I retrieved a piece of paper from my purse and called the wrong number. Several times I dialed the number for the mission house in Oakland, California, the place I would be staying on my return trip. Perhaps it was the distress on my face that prompted a restaurant employee to come to my aid. I explained my situation and he pointed out which of

The King of Kings and I

the lengthy phone numbers on my list was a Bangkok number.

After contacting the mission house, I waited near the safety of the restaurant entryway, watching for the house hostess to arrive. Relief flooded over me when a woman entered looking for me. I stepped out onto the street with her and we jumped into the back of a tuk-tuk, an open-air, motorized, three-wheeled type of taxi. The hostess's friendliness immediately had me relax. The tension in my body disappeared and although exhausted, I enjoyed our conversation and more sights of Bangkok.

The mission consisted of a few small buildings, arranged in a compound with a small open green space in the centre. I put my things in my assigned room and went out for a walk before venturing over to the dining hall and kitchen. I sat down at the large wooden table where I was welcomed into the company of several other missionaries as they bantered back and forth with easy laughter. Like me they were in transition, heading off in the next day or two to a different part of the country or to a different country altogether. Being the youngest at the table and not knowing anyone, I barely entered into the conversations. The hostess brought in a large plate of unrecognizable fruit. Without hesitation hands around the table reached out, except for mine. For me, eating the fruit meant one more adventure into the unknown and I was too exhausted. I needed sleep and soon excused myself.

I walked the sidewalk along the darkening central courtyard. The sun sets early and quickly in the tropics. At this time in Calgary, nearing the summer solstice, I could still enjoy at least another four and a half hours of evening light. But not here. I reached my room, appreciating the simplicity of it, furnished as it was with the basic bed, dresser, table, and chair, a combination of dark wood and bamboo. There was no need to unpack since I was leaving Bangkok the next day for a twenty-hour train ride to the south of the country.

In the darkness of my room, I tried to sleep, but the darkness was too dark. No light came through the one small window up high. No evidence of street lights or neon signs, only darkness. The screened window allowed in the constant noise of the Bangkok night. The rhythmic clanking of the ceiling fan added even more noise, but I knew that if I turned it off, I would not survive the night in the muggy humidity.

I peeked outside my door, half expecting the cool air of a Calgary summer night to bring relief. I looked across the grassy area toward the common dining hall, now dark. Everyone had retreated to their rooms. I closed my door to remain where I was, longing to be somewhere else—anywhere else. I turned the light on to dispel the darkness. But what good would that do, when I wanted to sleep? I turned the light off. I felt a desperate need to escape. But how could I? There was nowhere to go. I didn't know anybody. I didn't even know the fruit on the plate.

I felt trapped in my room with an inner panic rising. I lay on my bed looking up to face the darkness, the noise, and the heat. Tears trickled down to my pillow but they led me to pray to God for help.

And He did. The sudden presence of God infused my mind and my heart, surrounding me in a calm and peaceful light. I didn't want to leave that moment, but God meant for it to be only a moment. Once again, I became aware of the clanking fan, the humidity, and the darkness. But as I lay looking upwards, a calmness remained in me. God had made His presence known. He was right in the room with me. Not long after that I fell asleep.

The King of Kings

God showed me that when I looked up from my bed in my panic, He was above all those problems. God is above everything and He showed me this at the beginning of my time in Thailand. Already, I was learning some new things about God, who is always helping those who turn to Him.

God had also shown His presence to the Israelites at the beginning of their journey. No sooner had they left Egypt than the Egyptians pursued them. "When the king of Egypt was told that the people had fled, Pharaoh and his officials changed their minds about them and said, 'What have we done? We have let the Israelites go and have lost their services!' So he had his chariot made ready and took his army with him" (Exodus 14:5-6).

Despite the miracles surrounding their escape from Egypt, upon their arrival at the Red Sea, the Israelites had arrived at a new low in many ways. They were at the Red Sea, sea level. From that vantage point, the only place to look, other than across the sea, was up to the surrounding banks. And when they looked up, they saw their enemy. "As Pharaoh approached, the Israelites looked up, and there were the Egyptians, marching after them. They were terrified and cried out to the Lord" (Exodus 14:10).

They, too, were desperate to run to a better place but were trapped. In all of this, where was God? "During the last watch of the night the Lord looked down from the pillar of fire and cloud at the Egyptian army and threw it into confusion" (Exodus 14:24).

God looked down upon the situation and rescued the Israelites by making a dry path right through the Red Sea. God is always above. Above our situations, our problems, our enemies. When we are at our lowest low, God is above, ready to help us.

And I

Hi Mom & Dad, Well I finally made it to Bangkok! I arrived at 6 p.m. and it was 34 degrees Celsius, 91 degrees Fahrenheit. It is definitely humid here. You're pretty well sweating here all the time. The room I stayed in had a huge fan in the ceiling. There are no such things as glass windows. Everything is screened. Bangkok (5 million) is known for its noise (no mufflers on cars, etc.) So it was loud last night but I got 7 hours sleep which was surprisingly good.

I will be going to S. Thailand this afternoon on the train. I had a shower and washed my hair this morning. Sure was nice. Will write soon.

I am assured & comforted by the Lord's presence with me! Love you both very much.

After that night, I had no idea that several times during my trip, the darkness and humidity would gather again in force and surround me in their claustrophobic grip. At first I expected God to rescue me as before. He didn't. But on that one night in Bangkok, He had prepared me, showing me that I was not alone. God showed me at the outset of my time in Thailand that He was right above me and I held on to this by faith despite my feelings. Several times during my two months stay, I would lie awake for hours during the night in the stifling heat and darkness, longing for morning. I held on to what I now knew by experience—God was with me. I would always get some sleep and the sun would always rise.

CHAPTER 9
Advice Taken

Journaling, reading, people-watching, and gazing out the large windows across the vast rice fields and into the intermittent villages consumed most of my time on the train.

The train ride was about 22 hours long. It was quite fun but also tiring. I did not get much sleep because the train was loud and it kept stopping and going. When the train would stop at a station, there would be people selling fruit and meat to passengers on the train, through the train windows. All I bought on the train was a couple of cokes in bottles because I knew they were safe.

The generous amount of free time on the train allowed me to sit back, sip my no-name brand cola, and review my short stay in Bangkok.

After first settling in at the Bangkok mission house, I had ventured out at dusk to enjoy the freedom of a long walk after so much time spent on planes and wandering around airports. I strolled along several streets passing by jewelry shops and boutiques. I had no desire to shop, so I walked for the pure enjoyment of exploring this foreign city. In one area a recent deluge of rain, combined with poor street drainage, made it impossible for anyone to avoid walking in ankle-deep water. I thought it was great fun.

I later noticed a Caucasian woman who seemed to be following me. She looked familiar, and by process of elimination, I could only place her as someone I must have seen at the mission house. Perhaps she worked there or was a missionary enroute. She caught up with me, but not to chit-chat. She simply advised me not to wander too far from the mission house. Then she passed by me and walked on, leaving me a bit bewildered.

Why? What was the danger? Having immersed myself in mystery books since grade three, many diabolical schemes and plots came to mind. What part of Bangkok was I in? Maybe people got kidnapped or robbed here. Perhaps I was heading further into such evil depths. This place wasn't thriving with tourists. Maybe her comments were just a caution not to walk too far at this hour nearing twilight.

It didn't matter what I thought because unease had settled in. Having arrived on this side of the world for the first time only a few hours before, I chose to follow her advice. She must know more than I did, and I believed she was looking out for my well-being. I turned around and made my way back toward the mission house, but never saw the woman again.

The train finally arrived in Yala, a town in southern Thailand, where I met up with my friend David from my home church. It was good to see him again, and to be greeted by a friend so far away from home. I lightened my load by presenting him with the gift of the large duffle bag I had been travelling with since Calgary. Our church's missions committee had given much thought into what I could take as a gift to David from the church. Gift cards with their ease of transport would have been a wonderful option, but they were unknown in those days. The committee considered David's back problems, and decided on a foam mattress, tightly rolled to fit a metre-long duffle bag. It was light enough to carry but a little cumbersome, especially when trying to escape out of a bus.

At the Yala mission house, I met the superintendent for the south of Thailand and his wife. As various missionaries came and went, I was introduced to them, meeting some that I would stay with over the summer.

My huge travel days had ended. Now only short jaunts around the south of the country by taxi would be required to reach the towns where I would stay with missionary families. The immediate plan for me had been to spend that day in Yala and then move on to the coastal town of Saiburi where I would begin my summer work.

Kim Louise Clarke

As much as I wanted to begin my work, the advice given to me upon my arrival indicated otherwise. Someone mentioned 'dehydration.' I didn't know how I could be dehydrated when I had consumed two bottles of pop on the train. I didn't even like pop that much, but I'd been brave enough to indicate to the train steward, through my awkward hand gestures, that I wanted to buy a bottle. I handed the steward my largest Thai *baht* bill, hoping it was sufficient, and he gave me a pop and a handful of large coins, smiling at my surprised expression.

Once again one of the missionaries gave me advice. Stay another day to rest and drink lots of tea, water, and juice. Although I felt fine, the missionaries knew better and so I stayed. Throughout that extra day, I had moments when I didn't feel well.

> *It's now the next day, June 21st. Yesterday, my stomach was not too good, but I had a good sleep last night and I feel so much better today. Most of the travelling is now over with.*

The extra day spending time with the superintendent proved to be worthwhile. He explained missionary work in the south of Thailand and handed me a list of ten questions to answer over my two months stay. I hadn't known I would be getting homework, but my assignment was to find answers by having discussions with missionaries and discovering their viewpoints.

The superintendent also offered me a new approach to my journaling. Write what affected me on emotional levels. Write about the things I found funny, scary, disgusting, sad, and inspiring. He said that those were the moments that affect people the most, giving them a passion to express what they experienced. Writing would no longer seem tedious. What wonderful insights! I began a list of headings: Things that make me Angry, Things that are Funny, and the list went on. I filled the pages of my journal—pages that would one day rot in a landfill. But at least I didn't throw away the advice. The advice given me in the first few days after arriving in Thailand, I took to heart and it has never left me.

Several missionaries offered me information about living in Thailand. This would help me not to offend the Thai people. It was best not to question things too much, but instead to go with the flow. For example, don't ask why some things are so inexpensive in the marketplace. Don't question the drivers as to why one town's taxis are Mercedes Benz and another town's are old wrecks. When walking past a Buddhist monk, don't look him in the eye. In fact, being a woman, I should probably cross to the other side of the street to avoid the possibility.

I was advised to use my right hand when giving something to someone. The right was perceived to be cleaner because it was the left hand that was used for toilet matters.

I caught on to the importance of high and low. Anything of respect is placed physically up. One of the worst things one could do in this Buddhist culture was to point at something with one's foot. It was considered disrespectful to communicate using something so low and dirty. Such advice met me at my every turn as I acclimatized to my stay in Thailand.

The King of Kings

Good advice from godly people is one way that God, in His omniscience, guides and equips us. He knows what we need to learn and He positions experienced people to come alongside us. Our part is to be teachable, humble, and to accept instruction. "Listen to advice and accept discipline, and at the end you will be counted among the wise" (Proverbs 19:20). We want to be wise. And we know that not all advice is good. Through the Holy Spirit's power, we can discern the will of God and how to handle and assess the advice given to us.

When starting a new journey, we can be inundated with advice. Spiritual discernment is imperative. Scripture contains many stories of kings of Judah and Israel who at some point in their reign listened to bad advice, and the people of God suffered for it.

Young King Joash of Judah started out well, taking advice from Jehoiada the priest. "Joash was seven years old when he became king, and he reigned in Jerusalem forty years. . . . Joash did what was right in the eyes of the Lord all the years of Jehoiada the priest" (2 Chronicles 24:1a, 2). Joash proceeded with the momentous project of raising money to restore the temple of the Lord. Upon completion of the temple, the priests began offering the appropriate sacrifices. "As long as Jehoiada lived, burnt offerings were presented continually in the temple of the Lord" (2 Chronicles 24:14b).

Things did not continue well. After Jehoiada died, King Joash was on his own. Without a deep relationship with God, and no longer able to depend on Jehoiada as a conduit to God's wisdom, Joash failed. It's never a good idea to be so dependent upon another human being, since there is no guarantee you will both die the same day. Did Joash feel frightened or did he feel free? What kind of king would he now become? Since the devil never misses an opportunity, we should not be surprised that at this point ungodly visitors arrived upon the scene. "After the death of Jehoiada, the officials of Judah came and paid homage to the king, and he listened to them. They abandoned the temple of the Lord, the God of their ancestors, and worshiped Asherah poles and idols" (2 Chronicles 24:17-18a).

King Joash listened to the visitors and gave into the temptation of idolatry, dragging his kingdom with him. Because of their guilt, God's anger came on Judah and Jerusalem. "Although the Lord sent prophets to the people to bring them back to him, and though they testified against them, they would not listen" (2 Chronicles 24:19). King Joash ignored good advice. He even became cruel and had Jehoiada's son killed. That year under God's judgment, Arameans attacked Judah and Jerusalem, leaving King Joash to die of his wounds (2 Chronicles 24:22-25).

And I

All the advice given to me upon my first few days in Thailand was invaluable. And I am thankful to the people who shared their knowledge with me, showing their care.

Accepting advice involves humility. It is acknowledging that I don't know everything but want to learn. It is a desire to become wise in a humble way, rather than being proud and ignorant. "Do not be wise in your own eyes" (Proverbs 3:7a). I saw the importance of maintaining a heart willing to listen, and doing so kept me from experiencing unnecessary difficulties. If I had not listened to advice first given to me, not only would I have been proud and ignorant, I could also possibly have been an offensive, dehydrated, unimaginative writer who'd just been mugged in Bangkok.

Chapter 10
My Gift to Use

My short stint at the Yala OMF mission house eased me into Thai life.

I hope to send you some postcards soon, but Yala doesn't really have many, because it's not a tourist area. . . . Some areas look quite poverty stricken, others look quite nice. OMF mission house is right in the town and is similar to other houses. It's a normal wooden floor, and concrete walled, 2 storey building.

The breakfast I had was toast and a granola type cereal with nuts and coconut – delicious! Lunch is usually rice and vegetables and curried chicken. Supper last night was stew. Dessert is never cake or pie but is always fruit. Rambutan is a very strange looking fruit. It's the size of a large crab-apple and has one inch long tentacles all over it. It's red and green. You cut open the outside shell and eat the jelly-like white stuff inside which is pretty good! There are always lots of bananas to eat.

As I interacted with people, I learned to tread carefully when discussions turned to the subject of *durian*, known as 'the king of fruits.' It's like politics, sooner or later you find out which side people stand on. Are they durian supporters or are they not? The thorny spiked-skinned fruit, about the size of a watermelon, is cut open with a knife, and then pried apart to retrieve a beige creamy substance. Getting past the smell is the challenge to eating it. I never did get past the smell. Scientists have tried to determine why durian smells the way it does, a smell that can be detected metres away. Out of the fifty different compounds making up durian, it is believed that the volatile sulphur is what produces the odour. Descriptions of the smell include words like honey, sewage, cheese, sulphur, onion, and rotten eggs.

At the mission house, I learned not to delay cleaning up dishes after a meal. The exact second a dirty cup, bowl or plate landed on the counter, out from the walls through cracks, corners, and crevices marched the ants. How did they know? Besides the armies of ants, I also met shy geckoes and indestructible cockroaches. Thailand's wildlife was becoming familiar.

During this time, I read over additional handouts about Thailand. I discovered that the Thai population was comprised of 94 percent Buddhist, 3 percent Muslim, 0.6 percent Christian (Protestant and Roman Catholic) with the balance of just over 2 percent being 'other' which included Hindu and Animists. The list of OMF's ministries varied from church planting and language translation to working in hospitals and leprosy clinics.

Part of my discussion with the superintendent centered on five aims for the SPOT worker (Summer Program of Overseas Training):

> 1. Have a greater vision for the lost
> 2. Observe ways of evangelism
> 3. Broaden horizons through cultural exposure
> 4. Understand missions and missionaries better
> 5. Grow in spiritual life

If I did not make a point to target these five areas, I would miss out and be the poorer. I would neither understand, nor observe, nor broaden, nor grow. With so much input, I felt my summer was going to be an incredible enriching experience for me from which I would benefit personally.

In exchange, what would I be giving? Not knowing the Thai language limited my interaction with the local people since many did not speak English. My only special abilities were typing and crocheting and how useful would those be in the jungle? As a short-term worker, I knew that my main work would be to look after missionary children, so as to free their parents to concentrate on their work. I hoped I would prove helpful with more than enough to do and not be in the way. I didn't want people feeling the need to find me work.

From what I could determine, my spiritual gift was the gift of helping others. I loved helping out. So babysitting, for lack of a better term, fit in well with what I would be doing. This was a gift that I could offer. As a SPOT worker I would let the spotlight shine on this gift.

In Rodgers and Hammerstein's musical, *The King and I*, the British governess Anna Leonowens travels to Thailand, then known as Siam, in the 1860s. Part of her work included serving as schoolteacher and governess to the children of King Mongkut of Siam. This musical is based on Margaret Landon's novel *Anna and the King of Siam*, which in turn was based on Anna's memoirs and her account of her time as a teacher to the wives and children of King Mongkut.

I thought of Anna going to Siam to care for the king's children. I saw myself in a similar situation being in Thailand to care for children—not children of the king of Thailand, but children of the King of kings. These missionary children were God's children. God had given me the opportunity and ability to care for little MKs, and in doing so I could offer my service as a gift to God, a way to bring glory to Him.

The King of Kings

God asks us to give what we have. He has given us abilities and in return wants us do what we can in helping and edifying others. Our spiritual gifts, blended with our talents, abilities, and interests, empower us to minister joyfully. The result is a fruitfulness that glorifies God.

We never know where the practicing of our gifts will take us. "A gift opens the way and ushers the giver into the presence of the great" (Proverbs 18:16). Joseph's gift of interpreting dreams brought him before Pharaoh. "Pharaoh said to Joseph, 'I had a dream, and no one can interpret it. But I have heard it said of you that when you hear a dream you can interpret it'" (Genesis 41:15). Likewise, God gave Daniel insight to know and interpret dreams which brought him before King Nebuchadnezzar (Daniel 2:25-26).

Kim Louise Clarke

The practicing of our gifts may bring us into the presence of the great, like kings and pharaohs. But the great are more than just the leaders of the world. "Then he (Jesus) said to them, 'Whoever welcomes this little child in my name welcomes me; and whoever welcomes me welcomes the one who sent me. For it is the one who is least among you all who is the greatest'" (Luke 9:48).

And I

My ministry in Thailand would be mainly among children, in other words, I would be in the presence of the great all summer long offering my gift of helping people.

The exercising of our gifts will take us places. Not using our gifts will impede our witness and our usefulness in the building of God's kingdom. I didn't want to be an impediment in this great opportunity given me. "If we desire our faith to be strengthened, we should not shrink from opportunities, where our faith may be tried, and therefore through trial, be strengthened" (George Müller).

Ready to begin work, I stood with suitcase in hand in central Yala waiting for a taxi to take me to the town of Saiburi situated on the coast of the Gulf of Thailand. An old car arrived—not a vintage priceless antique, but old as in "will it get us there?" As I waited, other people joined me. It was only when the taxi driver determined he had a full enough load that he allowed us into his car and we took off. We arrived in Saiburi, having to stop twice on the way—once because we hit a goat and once because a hubcap came loose and rolled away. The taxi driver searched for the hubcap along the ditch and under bushes for several minutes to no avail.

I wondered if the loss of the hubcap was a big deal. We proceeded with three and the old car chugged along. An image crossed my mind of myself in Thailand being like a hubcap. Would it matter if I fell off the car and rolled away? But such thoughts needed to be dismissed. Hubcaps do make a difference. Their purpose is to protect the hub of the wheel from things like dirt, dust, mud, and water. I had a part to play in the ministry of South Thailand. My contribution would be important because everything we do in God's service is significant.

The Gulf of Thailand part of the South China Sea

BEGIN

Each new day is a God-given opportunity to begin again. Make the most of it.
                                    Dave Willis

You have brains in your head. You have feet in your shoes. You can steer yourself any direction you choose.
                                    Dr. Seuss

Chapter 11
Seashells by the Seashore

I arrived in Saiburi ready to begin my summer program where OMF worked primarily through the ministries of the Saiburi Christian Hospital. OMF began medical work in Southern Thailand in 1953. The Thai health authorities welcomed this outside help from OMF who had already set up health clinics and established hospitals in north and central Thailand. In 1960, OMF established Saiburi Christian Hospital in the coastal fishing community of Saiburi. It ran from 1960 to 1986.

The buildings on the compound making up the hospital were unobtrusive and fit nicely among the tropical grasses, shrubs, palm trees, and flowering trees. The hospital complex was large enough to house a pharmacy, laboratory, and x-ray department. Altogether there were forty-nine beds, several of which were reserved for patients with acute leprosy. Being a rural hospital, Saiburi offered help to approximately 20,000 outpatients annually.

For the duration of my two weeks in Saiburi, I stayed at the nurses' residence along with two nurses. Because one nurse was away on furlough, there was plenty of room. I felt instantly welcomed by the staff. Similar to the Yala mission house, the spacious two-story residence's main doors opened to a living room furnished with comfortable bamboo chairs, a couch, and a table. The kitchen and dining room lay beyond the living room. My room upstairs overlooked the side yard full of lush greenery.

Staff gave me permission to use the bicycle belonging to the nurse on leave. I biked over to the home of a missionary family each day. While the husband worked at the hospital, his wife cared for their children and studied the Thai language. My going there to look after their two children freed her up to immerse herself in language study.

After each morning and early afternoon with the children, I biked back to the hospital, and since the nurses were often still working their shifts, I would walk through the doors of the residence into a vacant living room. The aroma of simmering curry wafting in from the back kitchen always greeted me. Red swirls of oils, curry, spices, and coconut milk simmered in a large pot on the stove. Underneath the swirls lay diced potatoes, carrots, chicken, and bamboo shoots soaking in the flavours. Soon the aroma of rice cooking would be added. Besides the welcoming aroma, the quiet Thai woman who worked in the residence warmly greeted me. She was responsible for maintaining the home's cleanliness and tidiness and making these delicious meals. Most missionaries hired Thai women to help with the work around the house. In the Thai culture, the women were referred to as 'servants,' and they appreciated the employment given. If not for this opportunity, many of them would have had little choice but to be out on the street, with prostitution as their only income. The nurses, returning in their white uniforms, always spent time chatting with the Thai woman in her colourful flowered sarong before she left for the day, returning home to start preparations for her own family's meals.

Most evenings at the residence were quiet, providing time for conversation and time to read, reflect, and write letters home.

> *Mom and Dad: Saiburi is an interesting town. Lots of grass type huts. There are chickens and goats all over. There is electricity so some of the huts will have a TV antenna sticking through. It's quite a mixture of urban and rural. I've taken the kids down to the beach a few times. The South China Sea is so warm. I've gone hunting for shells. Every missionary here has their own collection of shells.*

I wanted to collect an assortment of seashells, but in the end, I collected eight tiny shells that when placed together measured one square inch. Having so few shells says a lot. It says that hunting for seashells did not become one of my priorities. So far, I had controlled my urge to shop for a new wardrobe in Singapore Airline blue, and now I needed to control the urge to acquire an enormous shell collection. Several times I had to remind myself that this was not a tropical vacation, but a mission trip. These months were not about me but about serving others, serving families and, in particular, caring for children.

One day I took the little seven-year-old boy for a nature walk. His keen interest in wood soon became apparent. As we walked, he gathered a fine collection of sticks, twigs, branches, and wood bits that he found along the path and near the beach. He added pieces of bamboo to his wood collection, unaware that it wasn't actually wood. The highlight of the walk came when he discovered a five-foot piece of bamboo deadfall off to the side of our path. He retrieved it and would not let it go, dragging it along behind him with the rest of his collection for the duration of our walk.

I carried some of his wood pieces, but also carried a concern about this long bamboo piece. Was it ok to bring home a five-foot piece of bamboo? I had no idea. This was a new experience for me, having never been a parent, let alone one who lived in the jungle. The bamboo wasn't covered with a thousand fire ants. I didn't see any cockroaches or spiders on it. There were no signs declaring the area to be a protected national park, where such things should not be removed. I was getting to know this little boy and knew his determination was as strong as the bamboo itself. I knew the boy's parents to be kind and understanding and, in the end, thought this probably was not a big deal. He dragged the piece up to the door of his house where he finally let it go.

It would have been a more enjoyable walk had I led this little boy to the beach to look for seashells—something I had an interest in. Free souvenirs for me to take home. But how selfish that would have been knowing he was more interested in walking in the forest than on the beach. This was his nature walk, not mine. My ministry was to serve him, not myself.

The King of Kings

That is how we serve God—by walking with the people He has placed in our lives. Some paths may not be as desirable as others. Maybe the path won't take us past seashells. Maybe the path is unpredictable or uncomfortable. But walking the path can be so much better when we are not focused on ourselves, but rather paying attention to the people we are travelling with. The path can even be enjoyed when we participate in it and embrace the walk.

"Everything if given to God can become your gateway to joy" (Elisabeth Elliot).

Pathway problems begin when our focus becomes self-centred and we realize what we do not have or what we cannot do. Then the path becomes arduous. We begin to grumble. The Hebrew word 'grumble' (*lîyn*) that often refers to the Israelites travelling in the desert has the root meaning of 'to stop.' This kind of stopping on the pathway is not good. It is not simply pausing for a little break. It is a 'dwelling, lodging, and tarrying,' even with the idea of stopping overnight. This kind of grumbling makes it impossible to move forward, because our stubbornness makes us come to a full stop. Our hardened hearts will not allow us to proceed.

In the Israelites' journey with God in the wilderness, their stubbornness and grumbling had them stopping many times. They could not move forward physically and could not move forward to grow in their relationship with God spiritually.

"When they came to Marah, they could not drink its water because it was bitter . . . So the people grumbled against Moses, saying, 'What are we to drink?'" (Exodus 15:23-24).

Moses knew they needed water. So did God. The Israelites complained because they only saw the path bringing them to bitter water, rather than to a place where God would show His provision for them. They saw the physical situation without the spiritual truth. Moses saw both and moved forward spiritually by turning to God in faith.

"Then Moses cried out to the Lord, and the Lord showed him a piece of wood. He threw it into the water, and the water became fit to drink" (Exodus 15:25a).

If our hearts are stuck in complaining mode about our lives, how can we go forward in faith? In our spiritual walk, we will come upon bitter water, and we will notice the lack of seashells, but there are other things along the path—important things God wants to show us, like pieces of wood.

And I

I thought tonight would be a good night to write because it's pouring rain outside. I am at Saiburi Christian Hospital for another week. I am having a lot of fun here. Yesterday we went

> on a nature walk but the little boy would not notice the beautiful shells, fragrant flowers, and many other things. All he looked for was wood! So we came back from our nature walk dragging sticks, blocks of wood and a long bamboo rod!
>
> Health wise I am doing just fine. I really like the food here. I am eating lots of oranges, even though the oranges here have green skins. Pineapple here is delicious. Dessert tonight was a rice and coconut pudding. (yum!).
>
> There is so much for me to learn here. I've been working on my homework assignment of 10 questions and reading some books. So I have lots to do but I have also more free time than I thought I would have. Tomorrow is my day off so I'm going with this one missionary to a market in a nearby town. I hope I can pick up some postcards.

I wanted postcards to write up and send home. I also thought they would make good souvenirs for myself. But postcards seemed in short supply. Travelling always has me looking for mementos—things that will bring back memories of my adventures in far-away places. My seashell collection did not look too promising. Then I noticed an abundance of coconut shells. The Thai people had many uses for them. Hollowed out halves of coconut husks worked well as lovely flowerpots and bowls. When I found two such hollowed halves I took them up to my room, thinking I would take them home as authentic Thai souvenirs. But the next morning I stared at the husks because they appeared to be moving. In the hollowed shells, countless ants covered the surface in a crazed frenzy. Unlike me, the ants knew that the husks still contained coconut meat in microscopic pieces that should not go to waste. Thankfully I had placed them on the floor and not in my suitcase. Once I had the window screen opened, I sent the husks sailing through the air, crashing down on the grass below.

At some point in my two months in Thailand, I hoped for an opportunity to collect or buy something as a keepsake and something to take home for family and friends.

Chapter 12
Painful Blessings

The running of the Saiburi Christian Hospital required five doctors, fourteen nurses, a pharmacist, physiotherapist, occupational therapist, lab technician, business manager, and three evangelists. Because leprosy was such a significant disease in the region, another four nurses ran the rural leprosy clinics.

Leprosy is a contagious disease caused by bacteria affecting the skin, nerves, and mucous membranes. It is a chronic disease that can cause great life-long disfigurement and physical disability. A sufferer will experience muscle weakness leading to complete loss of feeling in their arms and legs. Without feeling pain, open cuts and sores go undetected. When infections remain ignored, great damage occurs.

> *I've had a tour of the hospital and I will be able to go on night duty this week with one of the nurses to see how things are run. So I am learning a lot about the medical mission, especially about the leprosy patients.*

On my hospital tour, I looked into an open ward where patients lay on their beds recovering from various ailments. The height of the beds surprised me. They were fashioned to provide ample room underneath for a family member to roll out a mat and sleep. A family member or friend provided not only more care for the patient but also brought their daily food.

In a large room outside the patient ward, a cupboard held an assortment of woven handicrafts made by the leprosy patients. Bookmarks, book covers, placemats, and serviettes of light cotton fabric showed colourful threads woven in a similar pattern. Several rows of thread running parallel fanned up into pyramid or tree shapes before returning to straight lines for another inch, and then once again rose up and fanned out, creating a beautiful pattern.

The money raised from selling these crafts went toward the costs of the leprosy medications. It would be a few more years before these medications became freely available to those patients. I couldn't think of a better way to spend souvenir money on gifts for family and friends than by supporting the beautiful work of the local people here. Several times I found myself at the cupboard deciding which ones, how many, and who for.

One morning, a missionary invited me to join her on a rural outing. I hopped on the back of her motorcycle and off we sped. We slowed down while entering a fishing village, enabling me to take in the small hand painted fishing boats on the sand. We arrived at a neighbourhood of grass huts built on stilts among the palm trees. Two women greeted us as we walked toward one of the huts. The missionary knew them as former patients and they invited us up into their home. Out of the sunlight, the room was quite dark. The women brought out samples of their placemats, woven from colourfully dyed grass. I happily obliged and bought six rusty red and forest green ones. Such authentic beauty. These women's lives were pretty much a mystery to me, but I knew leprosy had struck their family, and happy moments did not easily come.

I marvelled at the local Thai and foreign doctors and nurses who worked with leprosy patients and their families, teaching them the importance of their medications and how to care for each other. The effects of leprosy upon a person, a family, and even an entire church congregation are heart wrenching. At the local church I visited, many of those attending could not carry a Bible because of what leprosy had done to their hands.

The King of Kings

Leprosy was recognized as an identifiable disease thousands of years ago in China, India, and Egypt. Since it knows no borders, the disease also became well known in Israel. Scripture records many accounts.

Uzziah, king of Judah, developed leprosy. One moment he

was fine as he entered the temple of the Lord. Then the next moment, when he chose to light the unauthorized incense, disaster struck. "He was unfaithful to the Lord his God, and entered the temple of the Lord to burn incense on the altar of incense. Azariah the priest with eighty other courageous priests of the Lord followed him in. They confronted King Uzziah and said, 'It is not right for you, Uzziah, to burn incense to the Lord. . . . Leave the sanctuary'" (2 Chronicles 26:16b-18a).

Then all the priests noticed something about King Uzziah which he could not see. "While he was raging at the priests . . . leprosy broke out on his forehead. . . . so they hurried him out. Indeed, he himself was eager to leave, because the Lord had afflicted him" (2 Chronicles 26:19b, 20b).

Many people contracted leprosy, not because they did something wrong like King Uzziah, but because of the nature of the disease being so contagious and affecting the nerves so that pain isn't felt. King Uzziah didn't feel the leprosy. He didn't feel pain. The priests saw the problem and acted swiftly.

Leprosy spread its way down through the centuries into the New Testament times where Jesus reached out to touch and heal many with the disease—but not all. Jesus's mission was not to treat everyone's physical ailments. It was to call attention to our spiritual sickness—our sin—often symbolized as leprosy. By dying on the Cross, and rising from the dead, He became the Saviour of the World, the Healer, through whom our sins could be forgiven, and our spiritual diseases cured.

Christ's intent was not to stay. After His death and resurrection, He ascended to heaven, returning to His Father. "But very truly I tell you, it is for your good that I am going away. Unless I go away, the Advocate will not come to you; but if I go, I will send him to you. When he comes, he will prove the world to be in the wrong about sin and righteousness and judgment" (John 16:7-8).

Like the priests alerting King Uzziah to his leprosy, the Holy Spirit alerts us to our sins, so that we may be healed. It is the Holy Spirit who proves "the world to be in the wrong" (John 16:8). The Greek word 'prove' (*ĕlĕgehō*) means to refute or admonish. The Holy Spirit refutes our baseless arguments about our innocence.

Kim Louise Clarke

Sin, like leprosy, if untreated will spread and ruin our lives. In making us aware of our needs, God knows that it may be necessary for us to feel the pain of our sin. God loves us enough not to shelter us from this pain, because He knows that it often is the very thing that drives us to Him for healing.

"God disciplines us for our good, in order that we may share in his holiness. No discipline seems pleasant at the time, but painful. Later on, however, it produces a harvest of righteousness and peace for those who have been trained by it" (Hebrews 12:10b-11). Feeling the pain of our sin is the first step toward our healing.

And I

Seeing leprosy first hand was like having a door opened. I peeked in and saw a world of suffering, something in my sheltered life I had not seen before. The haunting scenes of leprosy might blur over time, but they do not disappear. Three years after my time in Thailand, I wrote a poem:

The Leper

You are called unclean
You use medications and needles
A bacteria has affected your nerves
Damaged nerves have resulted in numbness
Complications brought on your ulcers
Your hands have become deformed
With stubs left for fingers
Your feet have lost their toes
To some you are repulsive to look at
Dark blotches have appeared on your face
Once a clear brown complexion
Blotches are seen on your arms
And have formed on your legs
I see you sit in the dirt and grass
Your back against the wooden planks
The sun blazing down on your dirty sarong
I see in your lap a book, stained and worn

The King of Kings and I

In awkward movements you turn pages
Pages filled with words
Words of such contrast to you
Words such as clean and pure
Whole and new, unblemished and unspotted
Strange words for you who is called unclean.
Called one of society's dregs
Yet, as you sit in the dirt and grass,
A look of hope crosses your blemished face

Historical note: Leprosy worldwide has seen a significant decrease because of medical advancements. In the 1940s the drug dapsone was developed, which proved useful, but the treatment needed to be administered to the patient for many years, often for the patient's lifetime. In the 1960s two other drugs were discovered and combined with the dapsone. The term was known as MDT, a multidrug therapy. In 1981 a World Health Organization (WHO) study group recommended MDT because it cured the patient and killed the pathogen. Since 1995 MDT, through WHO, has been provided free to all leprosy patients anywhere in the world.

CHAPTER 13
The Fear Chapter

A story from my Grade Three writing journal, entitled "The Coast," began: "On our exciting vacation which was all through Oregon, one place that I really enjoyed was the Pacific Ocean." Years later, now in my twenties, here I was once again at the place called the Pacific Ocean. Only this time, I saw it from the other side of the world. With its waters stretching across the globe, covering over 30 percent of the earth's surface, the Pacific Ocean is indeed a big place to visit. 'Big' is how God made the oceans! "There is the sea, vast and spacious, teeming with creatures beyond number—living things both large and small" (Psalm 104:25).

This part of the Pacific Ocean, the Gulf of Thailand in the South China Sea, although beautiful, is not perfect in our fallen world. 'Pacific' in Latin means 'peaceful,' but not all is peaceful upon the waters. The ocean stretches out to an ever-darkening blue horizon. A fitting colour when I think of the perils upon those deep waters. Since arriving in Saiburi, I had heard stories of what happened out there with modern day pirates, boats full of fleeing refugees, and rising storms.

It was at the shoreline where the sea holds warm shallow water that I took the kids. There at the beach they could splash around in the warm gentle waves. It was always a fun place to be.

One afternoon I went with the missionary family to the beach for a picnic lunch. We set up a green and white striped umbrella in the fine sand. For the most part, we had the beach to ourselves. A few empty thatched huts and a couple of picnic tables dotted this section of the beach. I didn't know if the little chalet-style huts were change rooms or shelters from the inevitable afternoon tropical downpours. We enjoyed our delicious Thai picnic lunch. From a banana leaf, I

The King of Kings and I

unwrapped the most delicious treat—a sticky rice cake. I had been in Thailand not quite two weeks, but I began wondering if I was gaining weight. Sweet sticky rice had become irresistible.

Other than the missionary kids, no other visitors at the beach ran around on the vast shores or played in the sand and waves. No one else was having a picnic; no one else was having fun. The local people simply watched us as they passed by.

> *Thai people that are walking on the beach will stop and watch us swimming in the ocean. They, themselves would never swim in the ocean because they are afraid of the water and the evil spirits they believe dwell there.*
>
> *A lot of little kids have a piece of white string tied around their wrists. The parents believe that this will keep them from having bad things happening to them and to protect them from any evil spirits.*
>
> *The people are terribly frightened by evil spirits, so that the cemetery is the safest place in town, because they believe that's where a lot of evil spirits live. Not even thieves would go there!*

The Thai people are predominantly Buddhist, but I was seeing a version of Buddhism mixed with animism, called Folk Buddhism where super natural power is attributed to natural phenomena, objects, or plants. It was easy to understand how superstitions had become part of this type of Buddhism.

The King of Kings

Superstitions bind many people. This is not something new. Isaiah says, "You, Lord, have abandoned your people, the descendants of Jacob. They are full of superstitions from the East; they practice divination like the Philistines and embrace pagan customs" (Isaiah 2:6). The key word is 'full.' The Hebrew expression 'full of superstitions' *(mâlâ)* is accompanied by the idea of being set, or satisfied, or even fenced in. This emphasizes the extent to which the Israelites, over time, had left God's teachings and had become fenced-in, full, and satisfied with the teachings from surrounding nations—the very teachings God had warned them against.

King Ahaz of Judah contributed greatly to this downfall of God's people. His spiritual fear had him trying to cover all the bases for all the gods, including the one true God. According to Ahaz, temple offerings in Jerusalem had to continue, at least in some fashion, because that was to way to appease the God of Israel. But he also had other gods to worry about. This had Ahaz treating the temple as if it were his living room, moving altars as if they were couches, rearranging them and even shopping for more.

"As for the bronze altar that stood before the Lord, he brought it from the front of the temple—from between the new altar and the temple of the Lord—and put it on the north side of the new altar" (2 Kings 16:14).

On a trip to Damascus, King Ahaz spotted a pagan altar design that he just had to have. "He saw an altar in Damascus and sent to Uriah the priest a sketch of the altar, with detailed plans for its construction" (2 Kings 16:10b).

He continued worshipping many gods in his own style, oblivious to God's laws and practices handed down through the generations since Moses. He did not understand the sacred meaning infused in Israel's sacrificial practices. These practices were intended to convince Israel, and through Israel, the entire world of their need for a Perfect Sacrifice, the coming of a Messiah.

King Ahaz ordered Uriah the priest to do things according to what he wanted and not in obedience to God. "Splash against this altar the blood of all the burnt offerings and sacrifices. But I will use the bronze altar for seeking guidance" (2 Kings 16:15b).

Ahaz moved the original altar and used it for divination, a practice performed in surrounding nations, often involving the examination of the entrails of sacrificed animals to determine the future. He was either ignorant of, or he chose to ignore God's straightforward warning: "Do not practice divination or seek omens" (Leviticus 19:26b).

King Ahaz's superstitions led him to commit abominable things. "He followed the ways of the kings of Israel and even sacrificed his son in the fire, engaging in the detestable practices of the nations the Lord had driven out before the Israelites" (2 Kings 16:3).

Being "full of superstitions" makes it difficult for anything good to enter. There is no room other than for fear to invade and take over. The *Oxford Canadian Dictionary* defines 'superstition' as an "irrational fear, especially as based on fear for the supernatural; for the unknown and the mysterious."

As Christians, the only fear we are to have is the awesome fear of God. This is a rational fear, not because God is unknown to us, but because He is known to us. The Lord says: "Should you not fear me? . . . Should you not tremble in my presence? I made the sand a boundary for the sea, an everlasting barrier it cannot cross. The waves may roll, but they cannot prevail; they may roar, but they cannot cross it" (Jeremiah 5:22). In fact, according to Proverbs, fearing God is "the beginning of wisdom" (Proverbs 9:10a).

And I

By picnicking at the beach and swimming in the ocean I began to understand an important quality to have if one is going to serve God. Fearlessness. A life without fear will be a life noticed by the world. And Christians want people to notice their lives only so that through their lives they can point people to Christ.

This fearless living can only happen when we depend on God and His power rather than depending on ourselves. Elisabeth Elliot wrote, "Fear arises when we imagine that everything depends on us." I saw how the missionaries choose to fear God, live with joy, and trust in Christ. A Christian's lifestyle free of superstition speaks to a fear-stricken world. Be free in Christ. He is the one who stills the waters—so come on in, the water's fine.

Chapter 14
Flowers

Every two weeks OMF nurses, Minka Hanskamp from Holland and Margaret Morgan from Wales, travelled to the town of Pujud in South Thailand to run their leprosy clinic. But on April 20, 1974, while in Pujud, they were lured away, thinking they were going to the aid of people needing treatment. Instead they were kidnapped.

It was an ugly time in Southeast Asia because of the Vietnam War. Many people fled their homelands seeking refuge in northern Thailand away from the bordering countries of Cambodia and Laos. In South Thailand, along the border of Malaysia, a predominantly Muslim country, tensions mounted among the Muslim liberation groups.

OMF did not get involved in political issues. They also did not pay ransom for missionaries, because this could open up a threatening situation for all their missionaries. Ten days later, on April 30, OMF received a letter from Margaret and Minka, confirming that they had been kidnapped. Another letter followed from their captors asking for a ransom of half a million dollars. Negotiation attempts, involving Thai officials, Thai military, OMF, and the kidnappers, took place but failed. Eventually it was reported that both Margaret and Minka were shot and killed. This was confirmed and their remains were discovered a year later in March of 1975.

At fifty-two, Margaret had been celebrating sixteen years with OMF on the day of her capture. Minka, forty, had served with OMF for nine years. Both women had a heart for serving Christ, despite the tensions in the country.

In May of 1975, many attended the memorial ceremony at Margaret's and Minka's gravesite, and many became open to learning about the faith of these two women. The quiet faithful testimony of these nurses during their captivity was said to have spoken even to their captors. The King and Queen of Thailand visited Saiburi, acknowledging these two women and the price they paid. King Bhumibol Adulyadej, a Buddhist, may not have acknowledged these missionaries in their service to Christ, the King of kings, but he knew that they had faithfully and sacrificially served the people of Thailand.

The King of Kings

The nurses' powerful memorial ceremony could have been encapsulated in this verse: "We remember before our God and Father your work produced by faith, your labor prompted by love, and your endurance inspired by hope in our Lord Jesus Christ" (1 Thessalonians 1:3).

Margaret and Minka, prompted by the love of Christ and love for the Thai people, served the lowest caste of that society. They helped them in their poverty. They treated the people's sores, teaching them about their medication and how to manage life with their disease. In doing this they unknowingly entered into a political situation and were killed. They were simply going about the work of the Lord.

That is what serving Christ is about—the continual faithful day by day ministering to others. As Paul wrote, "Make it your ambition to lead a quiet life: You should mind your own business and work with your hands, just as we told you, so that your daily life may win the respect of outsiders" (1 Thessalonians 4:11-12a). They were martyred for living out this verse, but the passage goes on to say: "Brothers and sisters, we do not want you to be uninformed about those who sleep in death, so that you do not grieve like the rest of mankind, who have no hope" (verse 13).

Margaret's and Minka's hope was in Christ. They knew what others still had to learn about eternity. "He is no fool who gives what he cannot keep to gain what he cannot lose" (Jim Elliot).

And I

Over the course of the summer I received several letters from family. In each of my mom's letters, she began with a weather report, because Canadian weather is always something to contend with. Then she wrote a brief update on the lives of my brothers and sisters. I had two sisters and four brothers, and their summaries consumed a good portion of her letters. She wanted me kept up to date, and she didn't always spare the bad news. I think she knew it kept me grounded, knowing that if I was struggling overseas, then being at home had its struggles too. And I think she knew I would pray.

In one letter, my mom mentioned that my brother, a city police officer, had to deal with a horrific accident on Deerfoot Trail, the freeway that cuts through the city of Calgary. Four young people had died. What a terrible loss of life. What a reminder it was to me of how short life was, whether a young adult in Calgary or like Margaret and Minka, missionaries serving overseas. And right at that moment I was both a young adult and a missionary—well, a short-term one anyway. My life could take a sudden turn or even suddenly reach its end. "The life of mortals is like grass, they flourish like a flower of the field; the wind blows over it and it is gone" (Psalm 103:15-16a).

My mom's letter was a reminder to me that each day is a gift from God. I need to value each day and live it wisely with purpose. And the purpose each day is to serve Christ. The moments spent at Margaret and Minka's gravesite reinforced this too. I saw that the cost of following Christ can be life itself, and that helped me understand something about the aim to, "understand missions and missionaries better."

The photo I took of the gravesite shows a rectangular headstone with a stone cross at its top. Engraved under their names are the words: "In His presence is fullness of joy - Psalm 16:11." There is a tree to the right of their headstone. The branches reach down to the ground and are covered in small, rich gold coloured flowers providing an aptly beautiful background. The beauty of the flowers will fade, like the earthly lives of these two women, but in Christ's presence, their lives continue with fullness and joy. That is the assurance we have and the hope we live in.

> *I hope you both are doing well and enjoying your summer! I will be writing again soon. I'm giving this letter to a nurse who is going up to Bangkok, so you may even get this letter before my last one.*
> *P.S. The flowers here are so beautiful. There are big trees with flowers all over.*

Chapter 15
Shake It Off

One evening in the nurses' residence, I left my room and walked toward the washroom. I came to an abrupt stop at the doorway when I saw a spider—the biggest one I had ever seen. Its body spanned nearly three inches, with another two inches of legs. In other words, it was a monster at least the size of my hand. It was not hairy like a tarantula but was a brown, bald, solid mass. When it moved across the floor, I heard little tapping noises as each leg touched the bathroom tiles.

While frozen to the floor, three possibilities raced through my mind—run, scream, or take a picture of the spider alongside something like a paperclip to prove the size of this nightmare. I chose the first option. I backed away, and then ran down the hall to the nearest nurse's room.

The nurse chuckled as she listened to me. She put her pen down and rose from her chair, leaving the letters on her desk where every week she wrote to friends and family back home. She headed down the hall toward the bathroom, with me following a safe distance behind. She explained as she walked.

"It must be a rain spider. Sometimes these spiders will come inside when it rains hard. The window must have been left open."

In the calm explanation, I detected a sense of sympathy toward these creatures, a sympathy I failed to understand.

As soon as she saw it, her suspicions were confirmed—a rain spider. She tried to shoo it back toward the window, directing it with a broom, but it wasn't cooperating. In the end it met its demise. The nurse didn't want to kill the spider, and even I didn't want to see the spider die.

These rain spiders, also called Huntsman spiders, pose no danger. Their bite may cause a few victims an allergic reaction, but it is usually not a problem for healthy people. When I found out that Huntsman spiders are among the largest in the world I felt quite vindicated in my reaction.

I thanked the nurse several times, feeling that she had saved my life. The problem now was that I had knowledge. I now knew what lurked out there in the jungle and I had seven more weeks to go. Until that moment, I had only to deal with mosquitoes and ants.

> *The grease stains you see on this letter are from my insect repellent that I just put on. It's evening now and the mosquitoes are out. Mom, I've been using your soap and aloe vera spray quite a bit especially on my legs. My legs are quite a mess because of the many mosquito and ant bites.*

With my eyes now having been opened, I saw the mosquito net surrounding my bed as a spider net. Tightly tucked under my mattress, the net would prevent spiders from getting to me. It gave me a measure of comfort. The net had worked well in keeping out mosquitoes—except on one occasion. I had fallen asleep with my elbow resting tightly up against the netting. This was equal to setting up a fly-in banquet for the mosquitoes to feast upon. And they did. I woke with an itchy, lumpy elbow. Thankfully I was taking malaria pills and had had all my vaccination shots.

The spider incident had me thinking about other creatures like lizards and snakes. I was not the only SPOT worker in South Thailand and I had heard about a girl who had found a snake inside a house coiled up behind a door. I had yet to encounter a snake, but I knew they were out there.

There are over two hundred species of snakes in Thailand. The common snakes are the Oriental Whip Snake, Copperheaded Racer, Laotian Wolf Snake, Indochinese Rat Snake, and the Checkered Keelback. Just hearing their names is enough to make you long for the Canadian winters where many such unwelcomed creatures are either dormant, hibernating, or dead.

I found that the missionaries have simply learned to live with the wildlife of Thailand. They take these encounters in stride but remain vigilant and aware of the risks. Most of these snakes pose little threat to people, with a few having a mild venom. Most snakebites are not deadly. The important thing, if bitten, is to have it looked at and take measures to prevent infection. Only a few snakes pose big problems. These are the pythons because of their size, and the cobras and vipers because of their deadly venom.

The King of Kings

So far, I had only encountered a rain spider and I didn't want to make a "mountain out of a molehill." I didn't want the encounter with a huge spider to darken my time at Saiburi or set me on edge. Molehills, those little piles of earth left behind by burrowing moles, should be easily stepped over.

Our mountainous problems are what should cause us to stop and consider how to deal with them. Do we climb up, go around, or figure out a way through? Whatever we choose, Christ encourages prayer. "If you have faith and do not doubt . . . you can say to this mountain, 'Go throw yourself into the sea.' And it will be done. If you believe, you will receive whatever you ask for in prayer" (Matthew 21:21b-22).

Paul faced both mountains and molehills as a missionary. I think some of his mountains would have been being beaten with rods, pelted with stones, imprisoned, and shipwrecked among others (2 Corinthians 11:23-29). But in maintaining a close walk with Christ, he kept going forward in his journey by faith, overcoming all these mountains.

Paul also knew when a molehill was in his midst. "Paul gathered a pile of brushwood and, as he put it on the fire, a viper, driven out by the heat, fastened itself on his hand. When the islanders saw the snake hanging from his hand, they said to each other, 'This man must be a murderer' . . . But Paul shook the snake off into the fire and suffered no ill effects" (Acts 28:3, 4a, 5).

The snake bite was deadly and Paul should have died. But he "shook the snake off." He was not going to die from a snake bite or from anything else that day because it was not in God's plan, and Paul knew it. Before being shipwrecked on the island, Paul shared a message from God with the men on the ship. "Last night an angel of the God to whom I belong and whom I serve stood beside me and said, 'Do not be afraid, Paul. You must stand trial before Caesar; and God has graciously given you the lives of all who sail with you.' So keep up your courage, men, for I have faith in God that it will happen just as he told me" (Acts 27:23-25).

"So keep up your courage." Don't let a snake bite bother you. Don't let a spider make you afraid. Although we sometimes get our mountains and molehills confused, God is always willing to help us get beyond both.

And I

One afternoon, days after the spider incident, tea was served at a missionary's home. About to take my last sip, I noticed a few dark spots swirling around the bottom of my teacup. When I looked more closely, the spots took on the shape of five dead ants. I scaled this down to a molehill. I put my cup down, remained calm and continued being involved in the conversation. The ants were dead, and it was too late to worry if I had swallowed any. It was a moment I realized that I was gaining perspective and learning how to manage, and that I might possibly survive the summer.

I didn't know if I would run into another monster spider or ever see a snake. I knew for certain that I would see more ants. Thailand has its wildlife and I didn't want to live with anxiety, worrying about what hid behind every door or what lay at the bottom of every teacup. These were not mountains. These were God's creatures living and dying in the world alongside us and I needed to respect them and to learn how to live with them.

My two weeks at Saiburi were nearing an end and I prepared to head inland back to Yala. The inland wildlife, I was sure, was just as healthy and active as the coastal creatures. But I was becoming accustomed to the exotic environment and acquainted with the geography. I had begun to settle into the climate, the cuisine, and the culture. I found the Thai people friendly, hospitable, and generous. I felt welcomed in Saiburi by everyone. The missionary kids were fun and the little bit of help I could offer the families felt good. My mission trip had begun well.

Buddhist statue in a Wat (Buddhist Temple)

OBSERVE

If you make listening and observation your occupation, you will gain much more than you can by talk.
           Robert Baden-Powell

You can observe a lot by just watching.
                        Yogi Berra

Chapter 16
Offerings

An uneventful taxi ride took me from the lovely Saiburi coast and brought me back to the interior, to the town of Yala. For the next three weeks I lived with a missionary family whose daughter was almost six, and the two boys around four and two.

> *The family I'm with now have 3 children. They are a fun bunch of kids! I take them for walks down to the park, train station and market.*

I now had an opportunity to familiarize myself with the town rather than just knowing the OMF mission house and its surroundings.

> *Some of the people live in grass huts and shacks along a muddy little stream. Sometimes there are piles of garbage right in their back yard areas. Some areas look quite poverty stricken, others look quite nice.*

The home I stayed in was similar to what I had seen of other homes, a two-story building with high ceilings and concrete floors, giving that spacious warehouse ambiance. I realized that I was unlikely to set foot on carpet again until back in North America. The clutter of material things would never become an issue here. The large front room of blank walls and concrete floor contained a few chairs, a coffee table, and a bookcase. Beyond the living room there was a modest dining area. The kitchen at the back of the house contained the basics of a stove, a fridge, and a small table. Underneath the countertops, the open concrete space provided room for basins, buckets, and propane tanks.

Near the dining room, the stairs led to three bedrooms and two bathrooms. The family graciously gave me my own bedroom, the one with an ensuite. By now I was getting used to Thai toilets, most being a hole in the floor with placements for your feet on either side. This bathroom done in turquoise tiles, had a toilet a step up from some I'd seen, because it could be 'flushed' by tossing in water from a nearby tiled reservoir.

As Thailand became more familiar to me, I kept in mind an excellent piece of advice the superintendent had offered: take photographs immediately upon seeing something curious, new, or interesting, because things can become familiar over two months. A four-foot pile of coconut husks at the end of the road destined for firewood is an unusual site for a Canadian—at first. As weeks go by, coconut piles become as commonplace as palm trees and less note- and photo-worthy.

> *There are a lot of pictures I want to take. I've been taking quite a few slides. But I'm using David's good camera (a bit complicated) so I hope they will turn out ok. My little Kodak isn't very good for slides but it's simple!*
>
> *I've been writing all kinds of things in my Travel Happenings Book!*

Caring for the missionary children kept me busy for the three weeks. Often we would hop into the back of a tuk-tuk, similar to the one in Bangkok, to get to parks across town. These roofed but open taxis ran everywhere in Yala. All I had to do was provide the driver with the address, but it had to be in Thai. Addresses were more like descriptions than actual addresses with numbers. Phrases such as 'across the tracks', 'near the old market', and 'by the cock fights' would get us home. At first I referred to a piece of paper enunciating each word, sticking to the script. Eventually, I could rattle off the home description without any written prompts.

Thai is a tonal language. Saying 'Kim' could refer to my name, a needle, or a light, depending on where the high- or low-pitched emphasis is placed. French words, that I thought long forgotten, often came to mind when I attempted to speak or think in Thai.

Despite these challenges I learned basic phrases and numbers well enough to get by.

I was well into my ministry of helping families. As the weeks moved along, I became more comfortable living in the Thai culture. The adjustments to Thai life that I first needed to make had become routine allowing me to relax and especially to simply observe.

In observing the Thai people and their way of life, I saw lives entrenched in Buddhism. This religion has kept its roots deep in the culture since its introduction twenty-five hundred years ago. Around 600 BC Siddhartha Gautama was born into a royal family in Nepal, where his father ruled over a small kingdom. Prince Gautama eventually left the sheltered kingdom to travel the world and search for the meaning of life. In the process he became known as Buddha, or the 'enlightened one' and his teachings are the basis of Buddhism.

In Buddhism, the practice of detachment is fundamental. It is believed that if a person is attached to their life through their senses, their rituals, and a belief in their own permanency, they remain caught in the cycle of birth, life, death, and rebirth. Their regeneration will continue based on their previous choices and conditions. This cycle is simply day-to-day living with all of its suffering and dissatisfactions. To escape the cycle and to reach the blissful state of nirvana, one must do as Buddha did and through meditation, detach oneself from the bad and even the good of themselves. Some view Buddhism more as a philosophy than a religion, since in Buddhism there is no belief in God or in a soul.

Part of Buddhism is the community of believers, where people gather together in their local temple. Most towns have at least one temple which is called a Wat. These gatherings are led and tended to by the saffron-robed monks. The Wats, despite some being small, are highly ornate with fascinating architecture. It amazed me that some of these temples did not collapse under their top-heavy chalet-style roofs. I photographed a temple that had main doors patterned with swirls of gold and navy. The window frames in green, red, orange, and gold stood out from this otherwise beige building. The beauty of the Wat lost points with me when I noticed that the roof's outer gold edging featured slithering gold serpents.

Besides temples, Buddhists also create tiny spirit houses, those that I initially mistook for elaborate birdhouses. These little houses sit on poles, just above the average person's eye level. When new homes, hospitals, offices, or hotels are in the planning stages, the owner or manager seeks spiritual guidance regarding the placement of a spirit house on the property. It is important that the main building not cast its shadow on the spirit house.

Once the small house is completed, the spirit Phra Phum, lord of the land spirits, is invited to reside in the house and to protect those living on the property. In this mix of Buddhism with animism, a small wooden figure is carved to represent this spirit and then placed inside the spirit house. To appease the spirit, people place their daily offerings of food, candles, and incense on the tiny porch outside the house. The people depend upon the spirits for protection. These offerings continue throughout the lifetime of the residents of the main house on the property.

The King of Kings

Buddhist offerings at a spirit house or temple are given in return for the spirit's continual protection and blessings. Buddhists believe these offerings and good deeds will bring good karma, which will help them reach nirvana. They hope for good fortune to come to them, or for their prosperity to continue. Some give offerings, believing the karma. Some give out of tradition and habit. Some give to please the older generations.

I watched as people entered a temple, pausing at the Buddha statue just within the doors. Placing their hands together holding a lit incense stick, they bowed and placed the incense in a bowl. Some lit candles. Others placed flowers. After standing back up and placing their offerings at the base of the statue, they then walked away. They never stayed very long and I wondered what each expected from this moment. Did it help relieve their fears?

I thought about my faith in which it is only to God that I am to bow down. "For the Lord is the great God, the great King above all gods. Come let us bow down in worship, let us kneel before the Lord our Maker" (Psalm 95:3, 6).

I thought about the offerings we give, and the good things we do and how they should be different. They should be the natural outflow of our lives. We should do them because we want to be like Christ. "Each of you should give what you have decided in your heart to give, not reluctantly or under compulsion, for God loves a cheerful giver" (2 Corinthians 9:7). God does not want us to give 'under compulsion,' which in Greek (*anagkē*) implies distress. God desires the opposite. We are to give 'cheerfully,' which in Greek (*hilarŏs* from which we get the word 'hilarious'), means to give out of merriment and willingness.

And I

People will give rice and money to the monks because they think they will make merit that way and work their way to heaven by their good deeds. They see the missionaries as people making merit by their good deeds too.

But this is not why Christians do good deeds. We cannot on our own merit, be good enough to stand in God's holy presence. But Jesus Christ has made the way possible. "All are justified freely by his grace through the redemption that came by Christ Jesus" (Romans 3:24). We are in error if we think we need to add our own works to what Christ has already done by His sacrificial death.

Chapter 17
Enlightened

Five of us entered the cave of the sleeping Buddha. David, two young adults, a boy about ten, and I had come prepared. Our flashlights sliced through the darkness and we began to walk around this massive cave filled with gigantic Buddha statues. This cave, a short distance west of Yala, is called Khuha Phimuk.

> *A few days ago, I went to some caves. In these caves are rows and rows of Buddha images. We used flashlights to get around. Bats were all over the place! People were there worshipping the Buddhas and seeking by incense sticks to get their fortunes read.*

In one of my photographs, a sitting Buddha towered over us, three times our height. Its right arm rested on its lap, with its fingers curving over its knee. Each finger, the length of my arm, pointed down to the earth. Its left hand, palm-up, hovered over our heads. I couldn't decide whether the slight curve of the dark-coloured lips hinted at a smile or not. The eyes looked down at the five of us standing below, dwarfed in its presence. A pale-yellow length of cloth hung over the Buddha's left shoulder and extended across its chest, reaching to its waist.

The sitting Buddha's impressive mass then seemed small compared to the length of the reclining Buddha that stretched nearly twenty-five metres along the side of the cave. I felt small looking up at the sitting Buddha, but minuscule beside the sleeping one. I would have fit within the length of its head. Closed eyes and golden lips adorned the sculpted ashen face. A lacquered robe of golden yellow covered most of the body. This sleeping Buddha may possibly date back to 757 AD.

Gold was the accent colour throughout the cave, in the sashes, vases, bowls, artifacts, and in the Buddha statues themselves. Gold is a special colour in Thailand. Siam, the country's former name, means 'gold' in Sanskrit. Buddha himself is described as having "skin of gold" and his writings contain many references to gold.

The hand positions of the Buddha convey spiritual messages called Buddha Mudras. The left hand that hovered over our heads symbolizes meditation. The story is of Buddha's struggles with temptations, and his ultimate victory achieved through meditation allowing him to enter nirvana. Fingers pointing down display the mudra of "touching the earth." This symbolizes Buddha calling the earth goddess as a witness to the moment his mind reached enlightenment.

The King of Kings

People want to have understanding and to be enlightened. But I question how that is possible to accomplish on my own, when I read in Isaiah: "'For my thoughts are not your thoughts, neither are your ways my ways,' declares the Lord. 'As the heavens are higher than the earth, so are my ways higher than your ways and my thoughts than your thoughts'" (Isaiah 55:8-9).

True enlightenment for us can only come from God. Adam and Eve sought enlightenment apart from God and that did not go well. "When the woman saw that the fruit of the tree was good for . . . gaining wisdom, she took some and ate it" (Genesis 3:6a). My ability to understand spiritual matters is only possible through God's Holy Spirit within me. "What we have received is not the spirit of the world, but the Spirit who is from God, so that we may understand what God has freely given us. This is what we speak, not in words taught us by human wisdom but in words taught by the Spirit, explaining spiritual realities with Spirit-taught words" (1 Corinthians 2:12-13).

Being indwelt by the Holy Spirit means I am privileged to know the thoughts of God as He reveals His mind to me. Spiritual truths can be discerned and understood, because this is God's desire for me in Christ.

And I

I watched as people placed incense at the foot of a Buddha statue and then left the cave. I hoped that they might one day become aware of the light of understanding that is available through Christ.

This is an apt prayer to pray for those in spiritual darkness: "I pray that the eyes of your heart may be enlightened in order that you may know the hope to which he has called you" (Ephesians 1:18a). 'Enlightened,' (*phōtizō* in Greek) means to 'shed rays, to brighten up and illuminate.' That is what Christians are to do—share the message of God's kingdom, to illuminate the darkness. "The unfolding of your words gives light; it gives understanding to the simple" (Psalm 119:130). Just like our flashlights shed rays of light into the cave, so are we to bring Christ's light into the dark places we go.

Chapter 18
Free Indeed

The largest concentration of Muslims in Thailand is found in the south of the country, bordering Malaysia where the official religion is Islam. About 80 percent of the people were Muslim, and 20 percent Buddhist.

A Thai Muslim girl working in a missionary home allowed me to observe one of her five daily prayer times. She knew I was a visitor wanting to learn all about Thailand. Facing toward Mecca, she spread out her prayer mat and proceeded to pray while standing, then kneeling, and finally bowing her head to the floor. I appreciated her openness in letting me observe her religious practice.

The Islamic faith has five pillars. Fasting, five daily prayers, the giving of alms, confession of faith, and the pilgrimage to Mecca, called the Hajj, when it is possible. My visit to Thailand coincided with the fasting month of Ramadan. Ramadan is marked on the Islamic calendar in the ninth month determined by the moon, so the month varies from year to year in terms of our Western calendar. Ramadan represents the revelation of the Islamic holy book, the Qu'ran, to their Prophet Muhammad, and this celebration is considered to be one of the holiest of the Islamic seasons.

Fasting is required of all Muslims, with the exception of those who are physically too weak, or pregnant, or travelling. From dawn until after sunset, neither food nor drink is to be consumed. The purpose of this fast is so that Muslims take time to reflect upon their lives in terms of self-discipline and commitment to their faith.

Being there during Ramadan I found both fascinating and difficult. The men extend their fasting to include their own saliva.

Nothing must slide down their throat. Many times when walking along a sidewalk, a man bicycling past me would spit on the ground. I soon learned not to take this personally. It had nothing to do with me, and everything to do with their religion and their discipline in following its rules. Often tinges of nausea came over me, so when I saw men lean over to spit I would avert my eyes.

A celebration comes at the end of Ramadan. A wonderful opportunity came to one of the missionary moms and me when a Muslim woman invited us into her home to celebrate the end of Ramadan and to feast with them.

> *We were invited by this one local woman to come to her house for something to eat. The people are celebrating today because it's the end of their fasting month (where they don't eat or drink anything between sunrise & sunset for a whole month). Since the fasting is over, the feasting begins.*
>
> *We went to this home & sat on the floor with rice bowls in front of us. But the people of the house sat in the outside porch. After we ate they sat down and talked with us. We washed our hands in the glasses of water put in front of us. Half the time I didn't know what I was doing so I just did exactly what the other missionary did! I sat the way she sat & ate the way she ate. A person must never use their left hand for eating, and you do not sit cross-legged on the floor. There are so many different cultural things to learn.*
>
> *The women wear long skirts (some silk), long silk scarves covering their head, and a long-sleeved blouse that is never tucked into the skirts but just worn straight over the skirts, and of course sandals. So that's basically what I've been wearing, except it's ok for me not to wear a head scarf. The main thing is not to let anyone see your knees!*

The King of Kings

Within these cultures, one dominated by Buddhism and the other by Islam, I realized how great my freedom in Christ is. "Through him (Jesus) everyone who believes is set free from every sin, a justification you were not able to obtain under the law of Moses" (Acts 13:39).

Kim Louise Clarke

The Pharisees did not understand this freedom. They persisted in promoting a barrage of laws that were not even God's laws to begin with (Matthew 23:1-4). When the Pharisees questioned Jesus about picking heads of grain on a Sabbath, Jesus reminded them of centuries ago when David "entered the house of God, and taking the consecrated bread, he ate what is lawful only for priests to eat" (Luke 6:4a). King David knew that life with God was not all about following rules. David knew the laws of God, he knew all about his own imperfections, but more importantly he knew God the Person.

And I

God in Christ came to set me free. "Now the Lord is the Spirit, and where the Spirit of the Lord is, there is freedom" (2 Corinthians 3:17). From 'freedom' (*ĕlĕuthĕria* in Greek) comes the meaning of being 'unrestrained, exempt from obligations and liabilities.' Our lives are to be spiritually unrestrained, and free from slavery to sin. "Be assured that Christianity is something more than forms and creeds and ceremonies: there is life, and power, and reality, in our holy faith" (George Müller).

The challenge of knowing freedom in Christ is to consistently maintain that freedom in daily life. By observing Muslims practicing their faith, I better understood how my life should reveal the freedom I have in Christ, but lived out in a way so as not to offend carelessly. Rules surrounded me in my western culture and now in the two religions and cultures of Buddhism and Islam. I needed to follow rules, but it proved helpful to me to keep the purpose of the rules in mind, and the reasons why I felt it honoured God to obey them in each circumstance.

Chapter 19
Marketplace Poverty

I valued my personal siesta times.

I have been feeling fine, although it's hard to sleep during the siesta time in the afternoon 2-3 p.m. I usually just read or write letters if I can't sleep.

During some siestas, I left my bedroom, and taking the stairs to the roof, I would find a private place to sit in the sun. With both my capris and shirt sleeves rolled up as high as they would go, I had a chance of returning to Calgary looking like I had been in the tropics. Leaning back against the parapet I could feel the sun on my face, something not to take for granted. Back home, for five months of the year from November to March, the cold air blocks the sun's warmth on many of those days.

Several times instead of having a siesta at home, I ventured out to a marketplace by myself. In the marketplace, I entered a vibrant colourful part of Thai life. The sellers displayed their wares on tables or mats on the ground. Woven grass baskets, overflowed with spikey controversial durian. The nearby merchants in bright shirts, scarves, and sarongs, smiled at me. The way some of them squatted on the ground amazed me. In perfect balance, with muscular legs, knees high up near their face, they waved to those passing by to come over and take a look at their fruit, vegetables, fish, or other goods.

The air held aromas of fruit, fish, and some things I could not distinguish. Cauldrons containing boodoo, soaking rotting fish, had me quicken my pace. The intensity of its smell had me write another poem:

Kim Louise Clarke

> Boodoo smells permeate the market
> The purple brew of rotted fish
> Piled durian add to the reek
> Some showing their creamy nauseous dish.

In an effort to buy a cute pair of pants for my little niece, I experienced the barter system. My hesitation in purchasing them had nothing to do with the price. I held out the pants in front of me contemplating their size. I had missed seeing my niece at her first birthday party in June and I wondered if these pants would fit her. How tall was she now? In the clamour of the marketplace, I tried hard to picture her. All the while the seller kept lowering the price wanting to clinch a deal which finally happened with me paying a very small amount.

One day, as I strolled around a large market, in the company of other missionaries, a woman passed by. She didn't look at me, but I looked at her. She carried the signs of poverty. Her shabby cloak couldn't hide her face and arms which revealed the horrors of leprosy. What grabbed my attention was her face. Her nose had become so disfigured that it no longer resembled the shape of a nose. I wondered how she could even breathe.

Still thinking of the cruelty of leprosy, I noticed another woman. Her eyes pleaded for money, while she sat, holding a toddler. I was told that the child is often there bundled up and being held, but not always by the same woman. This child who I thought old enough to be running around wasn't. The little girl's eyes had a hollow look. I thought about her life. What would it become? Overwhelmed by these and other sights of poverty, I felt such sorrow that I began to feel ill and I hid my tears.

My times of walking through marketplaces drew my attention to two of my homework aims: "grow in spiritual life" and "gain a vision for the lost". Seeing the poverty, I felt greatly challenged. *Why doesn't God fix it? Surely He can do something to improve these peoples' circumstances.* The pleading eyes, the outstretched empty hands, and the physical deformities greatly disturbed me. Their faces told me they were helpless, and I felt helpless walking past them.

The King of Kings and I

The King of Kings

I had observed the spiritual darkness both in Buddhism and Islam, and now I saw a depth to the physical darkness, as evidenced by the poverty that surrounded me. Scenes that could not be undone. How easy to succumb under the weight of darkness and consider the problem too big to make any difference. I wanted to see signs that the kingdom of God was here. But the kingdom of God is not a visible thing.

"Once, on being asked by the Pharisees when the kingdom of God would come, Jesus replied, 'The coming of the kingdom of God is not something that can be observed, nor will people say, 'Here it is,' or 'There it is,' because the kingdom of God is in your midst'"(Luke 17:20-21).

The kingdom of God cannot be observed. 'Observed' is *paratērēsis* in Greek, which means "to be seen in the physical sense." The root of the word means "to inspect alongside, to note scrupulously." So the kingdom of God is not something we can walk around and examine. "What shall I compare the kingdom of God to? It is like yeast that a woman took and mixed into about sixty pounds of flour until it worked all through the dough" (Luke 13:20-21). The kingdom, like yeast in dough, cannot be seen while it does its work. Yeast needs to be thoroughly worked through the entire batch in order to be effective.

I found it important to look into the darkness and believe by faith that the light of God shone there. God was in the process of building His kingdom. Christians were at work in Thailand and the kingdom of God was advancing. Churches were being established. Thai Christians were being trained and built up so that Christ could be known throughout their communities. People were getting medical needs met and learning how to care for their health. Leprosy programs were set in place to reach the main towns and the rural communities. The word of God was also being translated so that people could read the Bible for themselves. Christians ran youth camps to build up that generation. Students from Bangkok Bible College came south for training as well. The missionaries lived in the community so that in getting to know their neighbours, relationships were built. The mission work included ministering in hostels and schools, refugee work, and a variety of communications so that through radio, television, and literature, people could come to know Christ and His power.

Christ's kingdom was being made known. "For what we preach is not ourselves, but Jesus Christ as Lord, and ourselves as your servants for Jesus' sake. For God, who said, 'Let light shine out of darkness' made his light shine in our hearts to give us the light of the knowledge of God's glory displayed in the face of Christ" (2 Corinthians 4:5-6).

And I

On my photocopied hand-drawn map, the dots and lines that I took little notice of before, I now studied with new interest. Seven towns and district centres at the southern tip of Thailand showed where OMF had established a presence. And because of their presence, lives were being changed. I heard of a girl who had escaped from pirates, and after reaching the shore, received physical and emotional help at the Saiburi hospital. She also came to know Jesus Christ personally so she could experience the healing that only Christ can provide to horrendously broken lives. God's kingdom is advancing.

The physical and spiritual needs were great, and I could have become quite depressed if that was all I saw. I needed to look at the suffering in light of Christ's mission. I needed to remember the work being done by the entire church body. The Christian life is lived by faith and so it helped to look at the unseen; the power of the Holy Spirit working in people's lives as the Word of God goes out.

I needed time to process all the things I observed. There was too little time for that but writing about these events and feelings helped begin the process, which also included some observations I made about myself. These experiences needed to find their way into my life so that I too would be changed.

Questions floated around in my mind. *What am I going to do with what I have seen, with what I now know about the world? How can I help? What should I do with my life that will make a positive difference?* Travelling should change people. I took comfort in knowing that it was changing me.

A typical Thai kitchen

STRUGGLE

The struggle of life is one of our greatest blessings. It makes us patient, sensitive, and God-like. It teaches us that although the world is full of suffering, it is also full of the overcoming of it.
                                Helen Keller

Grow through what you go through.
                                Keith Craft

Chapter 20
Appearances

Not far away stood an ice cream vendor. The three children and I had walked around one of the largest parks in Yala, and buying ice cream seemed the next logical thing to do. In the other direction not far from us, a group of about twenty uniformed school children had just been dismissed by their teachers and given free reign in the park. I watched them break rank and stampede toward the ice cream vendor.

This was hardly a surprise. In the heat of the day, what kids would not want ice cream? But the children didn't stop at the ice cream vendor. They kept running—straight toward us. I picked up the trembling two-year-old and held onto the hand of the terror-stricken three-year-old, and the six-year-old clung to my side as the stampede advanced. They swarmed around us. Some children reached out to touch the blonde hair that fascinated them. Others touched a white-skinned arm. Those not able to get close enough to touch showed their enthusiasm with their smiles, laughter, and excited outbursts.

We slowly made our way through the surrounding children and left the park. We never did have ice cream that day.

What a cultural eye-opener! These Thai children had no intention of scaring us. Their swarming expressed their friendliness, happiness, excitement, and acceptance. I saw first-hand the challenges that missionaries face serving God in foreign places. It's not always easy for the children. And I began to see in Thailand that a person's skin colour is a very big deal.

> *Because I am a foreigner I am constantly stared at. Foreigners are rare. So when I walk down the street with a missionary, people on*

The King of Kings and I

both sides of the street will literally stop what they are doing and watch us. They especially like looking at the kids (all have blonde hair). They want to tussle their hair, pinch their cheeks. They are just fascinated by them."

On another day, a conversation in Thai took place between the missionary and a seamstress in a large fabric store. This missionary mom knew this seamstress to be very clever in making dresses. In such a kind gesture, she was giving instructions for a dress to be made for me. As the conversation ensued, I leaned on a counter and surveyed the colourful bolts of fabric around the store. I noticed a young employee further down, behind the counter staring at me. As if having found courage she then approached me, and saying something in Thai, she pointed to my finger. Realizing that I didn't understand, she lifted my baby finger resting on the counter and said, "Beautiful."

Not knowing how to respond, I smiled and took my hand off the counter. I often found myself smiling in Thailand—it allowed me a few seconds to think of what to do next. This girl adored my white skin. What is it about skin colour that's such a big issue? Growing up white in a predominately white world, I could not relate to that struggle, but I gained an understanding about one of the world's greatest problems: how we perceive others who are different from us.

The King of Kings

After King Saul failed, God sent Samuel to the sons of Jesse to anoint one of them to become the next king. Samuel saw Eliab, and thought he must be the one. "But the Lord said to Samuel, 'Do not consider his appearance or his height, for I have rejected him. The Lord does not look at the things people look at. People look at the outward appearance, but the Lord looks at the heart'" (1 Samuel 16:7). God guided Samuel to choose David, because he had a heart that sought the heart of God. The fact that David happened to be handsome was beside the point. "He was glowing with health and had a fine appearance and handsome features" (1 Samuel 16:12a).

God chose other people for ministry who happened to be attractive, but their mission would have failed if not for their 'attractive' heart. "Now the king was attracted to Esther more than to any of the other women, and she won his favor and approval more than any of the other virgins" (Esther 2:17a). Esther became queen, playing a vital role in the survival of the Jewish race. Her heart wanted to do the right thing, which involved risking her life. The fact that she was physically beautiful was a necessary element to her story.

To tell His own story to the world, God also chose how He would look. It was essential that Jesus take on a physical body. God in the flesh. From a baby boy, Jesus grew up experiencing life in a human body, one that was not particularly attractive. "He had no beauty or majesty to attract us to him, nothing in his appearance that we should desire him" (Isaiah 53:2b).

But Christ attracted the crowds. The crowds loved the authority with which He spoke. The multitudes were amazed at His miracles. His close disciples, like Peter, saw something more in Him. They believed Christ was the Messiah (John 6:68-69).

Christ allowed those close to Him, who had seen past His non-descript physical appearance, to see a different side of Him. For the three closest to Him, the Father revealed the Son as He had never been seen. "His face shone like the sun, and his clothes became as white as the light" (Matthew 17:2b).

But the greatest challenge to Christ's followers lay ahead. It came on the day of His death. "Just as there were many who were appalled at him—his appearance was so disfigured beyond that of any human being and his form marred beyond human likeness" (Isaiah 52:14).

After Christ rose from the dead, and ascended to heaven, He revealed Himself to the Apostle John. Jesus allowed the disciple to see His appearance in a vision. "His face was like the sun shining in all its brilliance" (Revelation 1:16b).

The appearances of Christ tell His story. They tell of His humanity, His deity, His sacrifice, and His power.

And I

In my travel journal, I wrote about physical appearance and skin colour under the category of "Sad," but "Heartbreaking" would have been a better word. The darker a person's skin, the less valued they were in Thai society. The lighter a person's skin, the more that person was perceived as attractive, although this could create ironically dire consequences since it could open doors into prostitution. In the end, regardless of how a person looks, life will have many challenges because the world's judgment about people based on their physical appearance is usually harsh.

We need to be careful not to follow the judgmental ways of the world. We need to see ourselves and others from God's perspective. It helps to remember that our bodies are temporal. A new imperishable body awaits us (1 Corinthians 15:52). Meanwhile, we must learn to accept and care for the body we have been given. Our physical body is part of our story, to be dedicated to the work of Christ in the world.

Chapter 21
Time Well Spent

In addition to providing child care, I became involved in a number of ministries in Yala. I joined youth groups, children's Sunday school, and shared my testimony in churches and at Bible studies. For each of these ministries, I would arrive early only to find myself sitting, standing, or wandering around waiting for someone to appear.

Every day I strapped my watch to my wrist, usually wondering why I bothered. The Thai people approached time differently than I did in my fast-paced Western culture. At twenty-four, I had adopted a life style of arriving early to everything. Early for medical appointments, early for meetings, early for my own sense of comfort.

But I needed to adjust that practice. So I dropped my standards and began arriving on time. But this also proved too early. My standards sunk even deeper when I purposely set out to arrive late. Although it felt wrong, it worked better.

> *One thing I find difficult is that people are not time conscious. So things don't start on time. If someone is to meet you at a certain time, they'll meet you usually a bit later. It's hard not to do things according to the clock. Church starts whenever the people get there.*

Eventually when church services did begin, singing took up a considerable portion. One chorus in particular, "In His Time," was familiar to me, so that I could sing softly in English while others sang robustly in Thai. This was a favourite of the congregation, and once sung in its entirety, would be repeated several more times. It was no surprise that a few lines of Diane Ball's words and music stuck in my head all summer long. *In His time, He makes all things beautiful in His time.*

This chorus helped me deal with the categories of time. There was Thai time, my time, and God's time. I found it important to keep perspective on all three. As much as I reminded myself that this was not a vacation, I began longing for extended periods of time completely to myself. I reminisced about my walks in Three Hills, back in Alberta, from the school campus in town up to the actual hills the town was named after.

I especially wanted expanded periods of time for personal exercise once I realized that I was expanding. Despite being active, taking children to parks, and getting in short walks to the market, I was gaining weight.

> *Some of the things I've been eating have been very interesting: black rice pudding, black rice bread, coconut butter (lime green colour), coconut milk ice cream; pineapple skin juice, and believe it or not – bamboo! Pieces of bamboo were cut up and cooked in a stew. Tasted quite good. One of my favourite foods here is sticky rice cake, wrapped up in a banana leaf, and you dip the rice into a sweet milk.*

These exotic foods made eating a meal an experience. And once having tasted these unique and delicious flavours, it was almost impossible for me to resist more. The coconut butter was called Kaya, made with eggs, thick coconut milk, lots of sugar, and leaves from the tropical plant pandana. These leaves added a sweet flavour and accounted for the light green colour. The bamboo pieces were bamboo shoots from young plants which were sliced and added to main dishes.

There were other things I didn't confess in my letters home, but they remain vivid memories. Like the time I visited a market on my own. I came upon a shop that sold chocolate, practically a staple in my North American diet, and something I hadn't eaten for weeks. I bought a bunch of little bars. They tasted like wax, but I ate all of them anyway.

Little wonder I was gaining weight. Other than the chocolate and durian, everything else was absolutely delicious.

Kim Louise Clarke

Then there came a point where I decided to do something to encourage myself to stay in shape. I didn't have much time to myself, but I had a handful of moments. Waiting for a bit of time to pass so I could leave the house to arrive late somewhere, or just waiting for things to happen at home, allowed me moments when I decided to do sit-ups.

The wall between my bedroom and the children's bedroom had a window and curtain. Unfortunately, the curtain was on the children's side which allowed the curious children to spy on me. Not wanting to entertain an audience with my ungraceful sit-ups, I took my exercise routine into the bathroom.

The challenge of doing sit-ups in the bathroom was not the discomfort of sitting on tile, but in needing to be attentive to the turquoise tiled walls. If my elbow or a sweep of my hair touched the wall, I could easily disrupt the route of the ants. A continuous line of ants never ceased to run along the bathroom walls. They filed in one by one, through a hole on the far wall, and marched in an undulating electrocardiogram pattern, to the exit hole in the other wall. Matching their perseverance, I persisted with my sit-ups.

I was confident that once back home, I could resume my routine and the extra pounds would disappear. In the meantime, I didn't want my problem to grow. My temporary exercise conditions were less than ideal. *But why wait until I'm home to do something, when I could act in a constructive way now?*

The King of Kings

King Saul struggled with time. While waiting for Samuel to arrive, he could have found something constructive to do. Instead, when his troops began to fearfully scatter, Saul chose to do something destructive. He proceeded with the burnt offering when he had been instructed to wait for Samuel, who would be the one to offer up the sacrifices (1 Samuel 10:8). "Saul offered up the burnt offering. Just as he finished making the offering, Samuel arrived" (1 Samuel 13:9b-10a). Saul's disobedience to God spelled an end to his reign as king of Israel.

"'You have done a foolish thing,' Samuel said. 'You have not kept the command the Lord your God gave you; if you had, he would have established your kingdom over Israel for all time'" (1 Samuel 13:13).

In not trusting God, Saul forfeited his royal lineage. Not long after, Samuel anointed David who would become the next king of Israel. After his anointing, David would need to wait approximately fifteen to twenty years before he could reign as king. In one of his psalms, David wrote, "But I trust in you, Lord; I say, 'You are my God.' My times are in your hands" (Psalm 31:14-15a).

And I

Handling time is often a struggle. Generous blocks of it never seem to be available when we want them. Meanwhile we waste the short bursts of time that are available. But life is most often like that—less than ideal. And too often I wait for those elusive ideal conditions to come along.

The challenge of living with Thai time lasted the entire two months. I never did adjust to waiting for things to begin when I felt they should be well under way. But I believe I learned some things. I learned to relax, at least a little bit, with schedules. And I recognized moments of time that just hung in the air, like ripe fruit waiting to be picked. I took hold of some of those moments and spent them well. The moments when waiting for other people, waiting for things to begin, or even waiting upon God for Him to show me the way, are valuable moments. How I use them is like a test. What will I choose to do with those moments? Will I use them well?

Chapter 22
Somewhere Else

With its hills and towering palms, the jungle faithfully closed in around me, as if to keep me tucked under its heat every day and every evening. The jungle kept the sky small and the stars difficult to see. In Thailand the sun sets around 6:00 every evening and darkness closes in fast. In the darkness one evening, the family and I headed to a street vendor for a special treat. We ordered beans in a bowl—a popular dessert of black beans in a sweet coconut milk. The beans were delicious, but to me the adventure was more than enjoying another food experience. It was about being out at night, having fun, and sharing in the excitement of the children.

Going out in the evening rarely happened in Thailand. For a missionary family, evenings were usually spent inside, preparing for the next day's work, reading, relaxing, and tucking the children into bed. The nightlife was left to those going to nightclubs and cockfights, neither of which interested me. But remaining inside during the evenings for me was a struggle. In the two months there, I could not detect any change in the amount of daylight. In Thailand, there is about an hour and a half more daylight in June than in December. In Calgary, there are almost nine hours more daylight in June than in December. I struggled with the difference, suffering a touch of cabin fever in July.

This mission was covering most of my summer. I missed being outside, which is what Canadian summers are all about—being out in the late hours of evening light if only because you could, no longer trapped inside because of the darkness and winter cold. The summer skies are big and the early evening air carries the aromas of barbequed meat and freshly mown grass. The days extend into the late evening hours until the sun slowly sets around 10:00, refusing to let go of its pink and orange streaks on the western horizon till 11:00 p.m.

The intensity of my longing to be outside surprised me. Letters from my Mom helped bridge the distance when I felt homesick. In fact, most news from home became thrilling even if it was about something of little interest to me—like gardening.

> *I have to do beets and spinach from the garden today. We picked the first ripe raspberries yesterday. I am trying to keep ahead of the garden as it is starting to produce a lot. Your Dad is painting the garage, keeping weeds down and working in the shop.*

Reading about raspberries and spinach had me back home for a moment. This became too exciting to keep to myself, and I shared this wonderful news with any missionary I could find. They were extraordinarily patient with me and politely listened as I describe my parents' garden. Perhaps I took some of them back to when they first arrived in Thailand and received news from home.

A mini weather report found its way into many of my Mom's paragraphs. She wrote about visiting relatives:

> *It was really cold, we just managed to eat outside and then the cold drove us all into the house. But we had a nice visit.*

Mom wrote about going to my sister's house:

> *We have had quite a bit of rain but further north they have had a lot . . . Their garden was completely under water and their house was like an island.*

And about life at their place:

> *The garden looks good but seems to be a bit slow. It has been cold. We wore our winter coats most of the time while out fishing.*

Typical weather. The driving cold, the flooding rains, and

winter coats in July. But none of that mattered because that was home. That was my Canadian summer and I was missing it. Along with those cold days, I knew I was missing many sunny warm ones. But it was my family that I was missing the most.

Despite my struggles, I never entertained the thought of packing up and returning home early. I didn't want to. I knew my time in Thailand was all too short. Despite the homesickness, I was having the adventure of my life. All too soon, I would be back home, sitting at a desk, doing research, writing papers, and gazing out at the prairie fields wondering why I had ever wanted to get home so fast. Once settled back into my routine, its imperfections and struggles would soon begin to wear on me. I would begin to desire a change from the ordinary. I would begin to dream of travel to somewhere exciting, seeking out something different, something more.

The King of Kings

When we are away from home, we can begin to yearn for its familiarity. Then once home, we yearn for something more. I believe we yearn for something more because there is more. We long for something better because something better exists. I believe that there is a place, a time, and a life that are meant for us. Jesus said, "My kingdom is not of this world. If it were, my servants would fight to prevent my arrest by the Jewish leaders. But now my kingdom is from another place" (John 18:36).

We long to live in the kingdom from another place, a kingdom we were created for.

Jesus longs for this too, when believers will be with Him. "Father, I want those you have given me to be with me where I am, and to see my glory, the glory you have given me because you loved me before the creation of the world" (John 17:24).

Many of God's people believed that something better than their current home existed. "All these people were still living by faith when they died. They did not receive the things promised; they only saw them from a distance . . . they were longing for a better country—a heavenly one" (Hebrews 11:13a, 16 a).

And I

Sometimes I get a sense of wanting to be somewhere else, even when my life is going well. It is an exciting place that remains elusive and yet faintly familiar. I get that feeling sometimes on warm summer evenings back home. It's the time when the sun is about to set, but the cloudless skies are still light. The air is fresh, cool, and still. In fact everything is still. And for a moment the air holds a sense of eternity where all creation is restored, beautiful, and exciting. That's what I believe this 'feeling' to be—a sense of eternity. "He has made everything beautiful in its time. He has also set eternity in the human heart; yet no one can fathom what God has done from beginning to end" (Ecclesiastes 3:11).

> *Thank you so much for your letter! It was great to hear from you and it meant a lot to me. . . . The time is really going by quite fast. I guess pretty soon I'll be back at school. I am looking forward to that. So take care & I will write again very soon. I love all of you & miss you all.*

Chapter 23
Travelling Sounds

The Thai national anthem, known as "Phleng Chat Thai," is heard throughout the country every day at 8:00 a.m. and 6:00 p.m. It is almost impossible not to hear it since it is played on national television, radio stations, and throughout the government loud speaker systems set up at train stations, parks, markets, basically any public space. Hearing it causes a standstill. Thai citizens stop what they are doing and stand respectfully still until the anthem is finished.

Early one morning a missionary and I were bicycling through the noisy congested centre of town when the anthem came on. This was nothing new to the missionary and she stopped immediately. I tried to do the same but struggled awkwardly, barely managing to keep my bicycle from crashing on the pavement. The difficulty after that was for both of us to keep from giggling until the anthem finished.

After the anthem, the familiar traffic noise resumed with the sounds of bicycles, scooters, and cars surrounding us. By now I was used to the traffic noise, far more intense than in Calgary. The vehicles on Thai roads seemed to have a life all their own, with their engines roaring and their horns honking incessantly, making every hour sound like rush hour.

My first night in South Thailand I wrote about another noise.

> *Believe it or not across from the OMF house is a nightclub. So every nite you hear their music which is weird and strange. I was quite tired last nite so nothing kept me awake.*

The music was not rock, disco, country, or classic. To me it was simply new and foreign.

But all these sounds of Thailand gradually became familiar,

including a noisy rooster that lived next door. Between the missionary's home and their neighbour lay a small open grassy area. I would often look down from my bedroom window and watch the neighbours busy with their cabinet-making business. Cabinet shelves, drawers, and doors would be carried back and forth between the field and their building. The rooster strutted among the pieces, incessantly crowing throughout the day.

The sun has been up now for three hours but the rooster next door insists on crowing still!

The sounds of Thailand—the national anthem, the traffic, the foreign music, and the tireless rooster—became expected. Whether I liked them or not, I could count on them and the noises no longer surprised me.

The King of Kings

Common noises of the day surround us. We expect them and we easily carry on with our daily routine in their midst. But I wonder how it was for Peter every time he heard a rooster crow. "Immediately a rooster crowed. Then Peter remembered the word Jesus had spoken: 'Before the rooster crows, you will disown me three times.' And he went outside and wept bitterly" (Matthew 26:74b-75). Peter may have heard roosters crowing every day for the rest of his life. How would he have coped hearing that sound that once had him weeping so bitterly?

Sounds can take us straight to memories stored deep in our subconscious. Some of those memories are ones we would rather not have. The past has its pain. The painful past can be decades old, or as recent as yesterday. And yet simply hearing a sound, a song, a voice, can march us right back to our mistake, our misjudgment, the words we wished we hadn't uttered, or the deeds we left undone. We go right back to our sin that has already been forgiven. We need to accept the forgiveness that Christ offers, and also to forgive ourselves.

To help deal with his painful past, Peter couldn't meditate on verses such as "Therefore, there is no condemnation for those who are in Christ Jesus because through Christ Jesus the law of the Spirit who gives life has set you free from the law of sin and death" (Romans 8:1-2). But Peter could remember back to being in the very presence of the risen Christ, when he sat beside Jesus on the shores of the Sea of Galilee being face to face with Him, and hearing from the lips of Christ the words that reinstated him. Peter was not condemned. He was forgiven and free (John 21:he15-19). Perhaps every time he heard a rooster crow, he would focus on his encounters with the risen Christ, and not the Christ about to be crucified whom he had refused to acknowledge.

The word 'rooster' (*alĕktōr* in Greek) means 'cock or male fowl' and is associated with the concept 'to ward off.' The crowing of the rooster may have been one of the four Roman watches of the night as mentioned in Mark 13:35: "Therefore keep watch because you do not know when the owner of the house will come back—whether in the evening, or at midnight, or when the rooster crows, or at dawn". The crowing of the rooster functioned as part of the protective routine for the city guards. It kept people on the alert.

Perhaps Peter used the sound of the rooster's crow as an alert, and as an instant reminder of the grace of Christ. When sounds take us back to our failings, we need to grasp the truth of the present so that we keep going forward. Peter didn't let his past and its failures hold him back. He went forward, becoming a leader of the first century church, and writing:

"Praise be to the God and Father of our Lord Jesus Christ! In his great mercy he has given us new birth into a living hope through the resurrection of Jesus Christ from the dead" (1 Peter 1:3).

"Above all, love each other deeply, because love covers over a multitude of sins" (1 Peter 4:8).

And I

Peter acted in faith and I need to as well. "Don't dig up in doubt what you planted in faith" (Elisabeth Elliot).

"For as high as the heavens are above the earth, so great is his love for those who fear him; as far as the east is from the west, so far has he removed our transgressions from us" (Psalm 103:11-12).

My sins have been removed. The word "removed" (*râchaq* in Hebrew) gives a picture of the area surrounding us having been cleared, allowing a great distance in all directions between us and our sin. And with such a distance, my sins are not available for me to drag around all day or for the rest of my life. No longer do I need to be affected by sins' weight. Because of Christ's love, I am free.

The local Thai Church

CONTRIBUTE

Every person has a longing to be significant; to make a contribution; to be part of something noble and purposeful.
                John C. Maxwell

We make a living by what we get, but we make a life by what we give.
                Winston Churchill

Chapter 24
What Not to Wear

Public speaking became part of my ministry which is best achieved when speaking about something you know and even better if it is something you feel passionate about. Since both of these fit the sharing of my testimony, my public speaking experiences were not too scary. At a Bible study and a church service in Yala I shared my testimony. Using a translator gave me that helpful pause to rehearse my next line.

At these gatherings I often met people my age and some whom I could converse with in English.

> *I went to the Young Peoples group at the church last Sat. night. Some of the people there had been in David's English classes, so I could talk to some of them. We had a Bible study and did a lot of singing. Since it was all in the Thai language I didn't understand a lot.*

One day I was invited to a high school to speak to their English class. Before speaking to the students, I visited with the teachers in their staff room. They were eager for me to explain some phrases in the English curriculum they were using from the United States. What was "bacon and eggs?" I did my best to explain this English breakfast, thinking that our language was difficult enough to learn without having to also learn about American culture. I thought "bacon and eggs" should be substituted for bananas, granola, and a delicious side dish of sticky rice.

I stood at the front of a class of about twenty students, talked about Canada, and answered their questions. Near the end of my time, I passed around a few photos that I had brought along with me at the suggestion of the mission board. The students saw photos of Calgary, the Rocky Mountains around Banff, and my large family. The only photo of the nine of us together had recently been taken at my brother's wedding.

After the photos passed between students, one boy having seen the wedding picture of people arrayed in fine suits, flowing dresses, and corsages, ran up to me. He kissed my hand, said something about 'Hollywood,' and fled out the back door. This had the other students explode with laughter, something I figured this student probably did quite often. My family photo didn't convey everyday life in Canada. The students needed to see photos of my family in casual clothes, like blue jeans, something fitting our day-to-day attire.

The King of Kings

In Thailand, there were no special events that I needed to dress for. But I did need to consider how I dressed every morning because my clothes needed to fit in with the culture. The challenge was to dress so as not to offend. What I chose to wear mattered depending on whom I was with. Wearing capris was fine in the company of Buddhists and Christians. It was inappropriate among Muslims, where I had to wear a skirt or dress to cover my knees; and where my sleeves had to cover my elbows.

We dress to suit the occasion. In the morning we think about our day and dress appropriately. Christ took this basic practice of dressing for the occasion into one of His parables when He spoke about the dress requirements needed to enter the kingdom. "The kingdom of heaven is like a king who prepared a wedding banquet for his son" (Matthew 22:2). This parable is not about just any wedding, but a royal wedding. People listening to this parable could imagine such an occasion calling for proper attire. Dressing up for royalty was expected, as both Joseph and Esther understood. "So Pharaoh sent for Joseph, and he was quickly brought from the dungeon. When he had shaved and changed his clothes, he came before Pharaoh" (Genesis 41:14).

"On the third day Esther put on her royal robes and stood in the inner court of the palace, in front of the king's hall" (Esther 5:1a).

In Christ's parable He reveals that someone unsuitably dressed at the wedding was found out. "He asked, 'How did you get in here without wedding clothes, friend?' The man was speechless" (Matthew 22:12). Consequently, he was thrown out of the wedding celebration. This is what the kingdom of God is like. It is a glorious celebration, but one that requires proper attire. The wedding invitation had been given to everyone, rich or poor. The only requirement was that the guests be dressed for the wedding to honour the king and his son.

Christ's point is that no one is capable of buying or attaining the proper attire. Only through Christ can we be spiritually dressed so as to be accepted by God.

"I delight greatly in the Lord; my soul rejoices in my God. For he has clothed me with garments of salvation and arrayed me in a robe of his righteousness, as a bridegroom adorns his head like a priest, and as a bride adorns herself with her jewels" (Isaiah 61:10).

People may try to get in wearing their good works and self-righteousness, but entrance to the kingdom will be denied. Christ paid the price on the Cross, so that the wearing of His robe of righteousness is available and affordable to all. It is free for us. "This righteousness is given through faith in Jesus Christ to all who believe" (Romans 3:22a).

And I

I don't remember the circumstances, but one day I accompanied the servant girl from the missionary's home to her own home. I walked with her down streets, across fields, past clusters of coconut palms, and into a clearing where her house stood. The structure was the size of a garden shed roofed with rusted corrugated metal. I saw wood and bits of debris strewn on the ground. At first I didn't realize that we had arrived at her house.

I waited outside while she entered to change from her usual sarong and top. It didn't take long before she slipped back out the door wearing a beautiful, immaculate dress. She looked stunning. Seeing this transformation from average to stunning had me wonder if she had a fairy godmother.

Transformations happen all the time. As Christians we all have a personal rags to riches story. Because of my faith in Jesus Christ, I have been transformed. God sees me beautifully dressed, absolutely perfect for a royal wedding. "So in Christ Jesus you are all children of God through faith, for all of you who were baptized into Christ have clothed yourselves with Christ" (Galatians 3:26-27).

Chapter 25
Building Bridges

Some days my responsibilities were clear. Without hesitation I would follow through with my plans and off I would go with the children.

I'm at the park now with the missionary kids, plus a bunch of neighbourhood kids. Once in a while I will buy them a Popsicle from the ice-cream man that wanders round looking for kids. I can buy 5 Popsicles for 25 cents which isn't bad at all!

Sometimes a day became a day off, when families joined together for the purpose of having fun.

Yesterday a bunch of the missionaries went up to a waterfall. We spent the whole day there having a picnic. Some of them tried fishing.
The local people say, if it rained the night before (which it did) then you won't catch any fish today. (We didn't catch any fish!)
Missionaries are always under pressures of one kind or another so it was good to see them having a break.
The butterflies here at the waterfall are huge and such brilliant colours.

Some days started off clear, only to become interrupted, like a dislodged rock muddying the clear stream. On such days, I needed to just go with the flow. "God not only orders our steps, He orders our stops" (George Müller).

One day a missionary had an unexpected visit from a Muslim man. I happened to be nearby on the main floor. He was invited in, and the social situation called for me to leave, because I was a woman and had no place being in the same room as these two men. I decided that the quickest way to disappear was to go to the kitchen in the far back. In retrospect I should have gone upstairs to my books and journal.

I didn't mind leaving for the sake of being polite to let people have their space and privacy for conversation. But having to leave because I was a woman was new to me. I needed to keep in mind that bridges were being built between Christians and Muslims. To do my part, I needed to disappear under the bridge for a while.

I sat at the kitchen table for about twenty minutes, giving me time to consider the life of the ant. Each of the table's four metal legs stood in a large can of water. I could imagine an ant's disappointment having reached the top of the can only to gaze down at a potential watery grave. Unless the ant figured out how to swim or build a bridge across the lake to reach the table leg, access to table top crumbs remained cut off.

Bridges allow access back and forth between the two parts, the two cultures, the two faiths. They provide that vital connection. So much about missions is connecting with people and communities, and then maintaining those connections. As a SPOT worker, my involvement in this bridge-building required me to be humble, teachable, and content.

I briefly met two other SPOT workers in South Thailand. We were on the same path to learn about overseas missions and to help out where we could for the summer. Despite the basic similarities to our summers, we each walked our own distinct path, bridges and all. No two paths were the same.

One of the SPOT workers had visited a rubber tree plantation. With a bit of envy, I thought about how fascinating that must have been for her. Perhaps that is why I wrote about trees in my letter home—a way of telling myself that I, too, learned something about tropical trees despite not having seen a plantation.

> *I enjoy going in the jeep, riding to these different places. It's interesting seeing the jungle. I can now identify rubber trees, sugar palms, coconut palms, beetle-nut palms, and banana trees! The people make good use of everything, eg. coconut shells are made*

into rope, bowls, flower pots and firewood.

The other SPOT worker, a young man, enjoyed outstanding opportunities, travelling by motorcycle to distant villages. I think he stayed overnight in some, being introduced to the village leaders and enjoying their food and hospitality.

God was preparing these two SPOT workers for ministry. He had plans for them and I had to believe God had plans for me.

The King of Kings

Jesus teaches us in a conversation with Peter, that it is best not to compare our path to the paths of fellow Christians.

"When Peter saw him, he asked, 'Lord, what about him?' Jesus answered, 'If I want him to remain alive until I return, what is that to you? You must follow me'" (John 21:21-22).

It's tempting when looking at people's opportunities to turn the question around and ask God, What about me? Why can't I visit a rubber tree plantation? Why can't I remain alive until You return? Why?

Jesus's answer leads us away from the need to know about others, to the need of minding our own business. And our business is to remain on the path God has set for us, despite having to live with questions left unanswered, at least unanswered to our satisfaction. It is called faith. "What is that to you? You must follow me."

God looks at our attitude toward our fellow workers. We are all working for the same thing—for God to be glorified as His kingdom advances. "Be devoted to one another in love. Honor one another above yourselves. Never be lacking in zeal, but keep your spiritual fervor, serving the Lord" (Romans 12:10-11).

And I

The Muslim girl serving the family, doing household duties, needed time off work. Sadly her grandmother had passed away and she needed to attend the funeral and spend time with her family. Without hesitation, the family gave her the week off. Who would take over the household chores for that week?

I really didn't mind the dusting. Dusting in these warehouse-type houses involved ridding the place of cobwebs way up in the ceiling corners using a long stick. I risked encountering spiders, but by the end of the week, I had not met anything startling. Because missionaries didn't accumulate endless knick-knacks, there was very little to dust. Vacuuming was unnecessary, but I spent time sweeping the floors. Most of my time I spent in the back kitchen at the ironing board. Each sarong, like a mini-bolt of fabric, lay flat across the board, making ironing easy. Shirts were another story.

> *This week I've been helping with ironing, doing dishes and baking cakes.*

It may not have been my most exciting week, but it became an important part of my story, my part of bridge-building between the two cultures. "Now fear the Lord and serve him with all faithfulness . . . But if serving the Lord seems undesirable to you, then choose for yourselves this day whom you will serve" (Joshua 24:14a, 15a).

Chapter 26
A Fantastic Arrangement

After three weeks in Yala, I spent a week in Betong, a border town edging on Malaysia. For over an hour, the taxi safely wound its way along the twisty road, between the words 'guerilla' and 'activity.' I knew not to ask why this taxi was a Mercedes Benz in mint condition.

In Betong, I stayed with a missionary family whose son was the youngest child I would care for. He proved to be a fun little toddler. Between his meals and naps, I helped to care for him as he explored the large world surrounding him. Everything and everywhere was an adventure to him.

Sometimes I helped out in the kitchen, squeezing juice from the coconut meat and stirring the pot of bubbling coconut juice, water, and curry. My help in the kitchen was more fun than work. I observed, tasted, and learned about Thai cooking. Throughout my summer travels, I collected recipes. I wrote out recipes for cakes, granola, custard, ice-cream, and of course, Thai curries. These I recorded in my travel journal, and this was the one page that I kept.

The heart of Thai cooking is the curry paste. People pass down their recipes from one generation to the next. Combinations of herbs and seeds are ground together using a heavy stone mortar and pestle to become an aromatic curry paste. A missionary told me the folk story that a man looking for a suitable wife would walk down the street listening to the sounds coming from the kitchens. If the pounding noises from the mortar and pestle were loud and strong, he knew that the woman grinding the spices would make a good wife. But today many women buy pre-packaged curry paste, making the finding of a good wife more challenging.

Besides helping out around the home, my week included travelling with missionaries into the main parts of town where their open-air preaching drew a small crowd. Drawings, words, and arrows filled the easel's paper explaining salvation in Christ. People gathered to listen and watch. I stood among them, listening to an unknown language, but knowing the people were hearing the gospel. I engaged in conversations at the Betong church, and shared my testimony at a Bible study group. In Betong I even got in some shopping. The missionary mom and I went into a clothing store where I bought two tops, happy to expand my wardrobe.

My week in Betong was my last stint of helping out families with child care. I had enjoyed getting to know families over the previous several weeks and having fun with every one of the missionary kids. My time looking after children could not compare with my babysitting experiences at home. At home I sat on a couch, with my homework spread out in front, but most of the time watching TV. A baby slept in a bedroom down the hallway, and I would regularly check to ensure he was ok. I made good money and thought the job was a fantastic arrangement.

There are differences in every way, when I compare my home experiences to my time in Thailand. In Thailand, there is no 'sitting' in babysitting. I looked after children throughout the day, and other than siesta times, the kids were wide awake and full of life. Although I had homework to do, it was the children that needed my attention. Time was not spent watching TV since missionaries didn't own such things. I didn't make any money, but I could not put a price on my accumulation of experiences and insights. So, was babysitting in Thailand also a fantastic arrangement? Absolutely—doing the will of God always is.

For a short time, I entered into the lives of the missionary family. I saw how being a parent carried many responsibilities. Beside the ongoing ministries to the Thai people, God calls them to raise up their children in a godly manner. "He decreed statutes for Jacob and established the law in Israel, which he commanded our ancestors to teach their children, so the next generation would know them, even the children yet to be born, and they in turn would tell their children" (Psalm 78:5-6).

The passing down of the knowledge of God, from one generation to the next, is far more important than the passing down of family traditions and recipes. The families I met dedicated themselves to serving God. They could have chosen a different lifestyle, but they chose to live overseas. They chose to live where cultural challenges, poverty, and even leprosy, surrounded them. I felt privileged to have met these people, and even to have helped out a little,

The King of Kings and I

if only for a short time.

The King of Kings

When I think of the families I met, one word immediately comes to mind—dedicated. Despite their challenges, these families persisted in serving God, believing they could depend on Him. What an important example so many people had been to me. I believe God wants us to look around at the lives of others, so as to be encouraged by their steadfast faith and godly lifestyle. God desires that we be dedicated to serving Him and when we do, we also become examples to follow.

'Dedicated' is also a word that comes to mind when I think of one of my favourite kings. King Jehoshaphat stands out because time and again he sought God's guidance. He trusted God, and depended on Him.

Before going into battle together with the king of Israel, Jehoshaphat wanted God's guidance. "But Jehoshaphat also said to the king of Israel, 'First seek the counsel of the Lord'" (1 Kings 22:5).

On another occasion when it was reported that an enemy army was approaching, the king's response was consistent with his faith. "Alarmed, Jehoshaphat resolved to inquire of the Lord" (2 Chronicles 20:3a).

When a Moabite rebellion rose, King Joram of Israel, together with the help of King Jehoshaphat of Judah and the king of Edom, set out to fight against the king of Moab. After seven days of pursuit, the three kings and their armies ran out of water. The kings' comments reveal their personalities.

"'What!' exclaimed the king of Israel. 'Has the Lord called us three kings together only to deliver us into the hands of Moab?' But Jehoshaphat asked, 'Is there no prophet of the Lord here, through whom we may inquire of the Lord?'" (2 Kings 3:10-11a).

Consequently, the kings went to the prophet Elisha. Before informing them that God would provide both water and victory over the Moabites, Elisha spoke sobering words to King Joram. "Elisha said, 'As surely as the Lord Almighty lives, whom I serve, if I did not have respect for the presence of Jehoshaphat king of Judah, I would not pay any attention to you'" (2 Kings 3:14).

King Jehoshaphat was known for his dependence on God and was well respected for it. He was not perfect but he maintained a consistent pursuit of God. He said, "Lord, the God of our ancestors, are you not the God who is in heaven? You rule over all the kingdoms of the nations" (2 Chronicles 20:6a).

And I

After a great week in Betong, I took another Mercedes Benz taxi back to Yala. This time I didn't follow the advice as carefully as when I came down to Betong. I got into the taxi, not having had enough time between eating and driving. Somewhere along the twisty road, squashed between fellow travellers, I felt nauseous. One man spoke a bit of English and I indicated to him that the taxi driver needed to pull over because I thought I would vomit. I expected the taxi driver to do this, just as my Dad would do for me when I was young and on our family road trips into the forests of British Columbia. However, the driver was not my Dad and we were not in B.C.

The passengers spoke to one another in Thai. The woman beside me by the window reached into a pocket of the car door and pulled out a small plastic bag. As if following orders, I immediately vomited into it. I tied the top of the bag, like tying a little balloon. The woman took the bag from me, unrolled the window, and tossed it out. From her purse, she took out a tin of creamy substance and applied a dab under my nose. Whatever the substance was had a strong but not offensive smell. It must have worked because I didn't feel nauseous again. These people were so caring and helpful to me, and I was so glad to be travelling with them.

We continued down the road when the taxi driver let out a sudden gasp. Everyone looked out the front windshield where a snake was making its way across the road several metres ahead. Its head was raised to our eye level, while the rest of its thick body slithered powerfully along the pavement, allowing the snake to almost bolt across the road.

I was suddenly glad that the taxi hadn't pulled over for me. There were things along the roadside that I would not want to encounter.

We arrived safely back in Yala where I would spend the balance of my days. My time looking after missionary children was over. All the children I took out on adventures had been wonderful. Before long, they would probably forget about me, but I would not forget them. They had positively impacted my life too much for me to forget. Neither would I forget about the kindness of the families and how each went out of their way to ensure I enjoyed my time. And I would not forget their dedication to serving Christ.

Chapter 27
Satisfaction

At the beginning of World War II, my Mom enlisted in the army and spent most of the war stationed in Vancouver, British Columbia, and Maple Creek, Saskatchewan. In Vancouver, she worked in an office administrative capacity at the Hotel Vancouver, which had been transformed into a government administrative building. She worked endless hours, sometimes finding only moments to exit the building to catch some fresh air and sunlight. Her typing was a valued skill and she impressed upon me and my sisters that typing will always be needed in the work force. Her desire was not necessarily that we work in administration, but that we pick up useful skills. All three of us have found our typing skills extremely useful throughout our education and our careers.

Being confident in my typing abilities, I was excited about my last week of work at the Yala mission house office. I would be typing up reports and assembling the program for an upcoming conference. Sitting behind a typewriter, I would be in my element.

> *Next week I might be working in the mornings over at the mission house doing typing, etc. So that will be a nice change. It will be about a 10 minute bicycle ride over, which will be nice first thing in the morning.*

As it turned out, my work at the mission house was arranged for the afternoons. I biked over, arriving early enough to grab a coffee from the large thermos on the kitchen counter. Everyone was on their siesta break. Sitting alone in the front room, sipping coffee and looking through the magazines, became my time. I enjoyed the solitude and didn't mind sharing it with the occasional gecko on a wall.

Kim Louise Clarke

I knew there would be differences between this office and the many where I had worked in Calgary.

I've been doing some typing here at the mission house. I guess I've been spoiled working in Calgary on a beautiful IBM electric typewriter and using huge Xerox machines. Here in Yala, I use a standard typewriter, and there's no Xerox machine so I do everything with a carbon copy.

A bottle of liquid correction fluid was provided for my inevitable typing errors. Similar to the familiar Wite-Out, once applied on the paper it dried quickly. I was told to replace the lid quickly after applying it because the fluid's odour attracted bugs. From past experiences, I knew what it was to be a bit nervous in typing because of a time restraint, or when using special paper where any correction would be noticeable. This was the first time I'd been nervous about a typing error for fear of a bug onslaught.

I began typing knowing my first mistake was imminent. When it happened, I grabbed the bottle and stood up, prepared to run. I dabbed the paper with the liquid and quickly tightened the lid on the bottle.

Nothing crawled out from behind the furniture or out of the walls. No ants, cockroaches, spiders—nothing. All clear. Feeling less threatened by the little bottle, I carried on typing. Each time I applied the fluid nothing happened, other than my mistake was corrected, and each time I was less afraid. Soon I relaxed into the work thoroughly enjoying it.

One afternoon, I left the office. Not having a bicycle that day, I began walking but my mind remained focused on the typing project. *Where should I put that hymn? If I put it on that page, then the Table of Contents will have to begin over there. Will that look ok? Or, I could . . .* Lost in thought, I walked along the sidewalk, oblivious to where I was. I could easily have been walking in downtown Calgary.

It wasn't until some men working on a building across the street called out something to me in Thai, that I snapped out of my office day-dream, remembering I was in Thailand. I don't know what they said, but I knew the reason they had called out was because I was a Caucasian woman.

The King of Kings and I

I'd been lost in something I found enjoyable and satisfying—office work.

The King of Kings

Our work can bring us a measure of satisfaction. If we know that our work is what God wants us to do, then I believe enjoyment can be found in it. That was how God initially designed work. Before the fall of creation, God had work for Adam to do—pleasant, satisfying work. "The Lord God took the man and put him in the Garden of Eden to work it and take care of it" (Genesis 2:15).

The work wasn't a punishment, nor was it arduous. That came after Adam and Eve sinned. "Cursed is the ground because of you; through painful toil you will eat food from it all the days of your life" (Genesis 3:17b).

Yet God still wants people to know satisfaction and enjoyment in the work they do, despite it being a fallen world. God's benevolence still abounds.

God desired to bless the work of the Israelites. "For the Lord your God will bless you in all your harvest and in all the work of your hands, and your joy will be complete" (Deuteronomy 16:15b).

We read in Ecclesiastes, possibly written by King Solomon, about work and life's pursuits. "A person can do nothing better than to eat and drink and find satisfaction in their own toil. This too, I see, is from the hand of God, for without him, who can eat or find enjoyment?" (Ecclesiastes 2:24-25). The Hebrew word for 'enjoyment' (chûwah) also contains the idea of 'hastening.' It is an eagerness and even an excitement that can be incorporated into the work we do despite the challenges that always come along. This type of enjoyment is from the hand of God, and in the true sense, this depth of satisfaction cannot be attained apart from God.

And I

For the entire week of working in the office, I found great satisfaction. It was truly where I seemed to feel the most confident.

I didn't know the plans God had for me after Thailand and Bible college. But God knows the plans He has for everyone. "'For I know the plans I have for you,' declares the Lord"

(Jeremiah 29:11a). He had plans for the Israelites in exile and I believed he had plans for me.

What lay ahead for me?

With two more school years left, I had not given serious thought about my life after graduation. At twenty-four I still did not possess a specific interest or passion toward a career. Was missionary life for me? Or working in children's ministry? The idea of "follow your dreams" was just beginning to saturate our society. But what happens to the person whose dreams are not specific, or who is yet unaware of their dreams? I liked typing, working with documents, and being organized but what kind of dream is that?

Hudson Taylor came to rest in God's will for him. "I am no longer anxious about anything, as I realize that He is able to carry out His will for me. It does not matter where He places me, or how. That is for Him to consider, not me, for in the easiest positions He will give me grace, and in the most difficult ones His grace is sufficient" (James Hudson Taylor).

Meanwhile, thinking about my future needed to be put aside. The immediate future needed my attention. It was time to pack. I was going home.

The daily busyness of Thai life

Return

There is nothing like returning to a place that remains unchanged to find the ways in which you yourself have altered.
                    Nelson Mandela

Travelling – it leaves you speechless, then turns you into a storyteller.
                    Ibn Battuta

CHAPTER 28
Wallet Woes

My assigned questions and the "Five Aims of the SPOT Worker" became part of the last discussion I had with the superintendent. But the final meeting in his office was not like a teacher reviewing my homework assignment, making sure I had completed everything. It was a wonderful conversation about my summer experiences.

Not long after the meeting, I once again walked by the market crowds to stand among the throngs of other travellers at the Yala train station. Gustave Flaubert once wrote: "Travel makes one modest, you see what a tiny place you occupy in the world." I felt that my life took up only a tiny space. So many people surrounded me, their lives big with challenges, some challenged with just seeking to survive the day.

My suitcase had become a little fuller than when I first arrived. The two new tops, a hand-made dress, some souvenirs, and the handcrafts made by leprosy patients took up whatever space I could find. I had my written updates on David's ministries that I would share with my church, and I had a number of addresses so that I could keep in touch with some of the people I had met. I said goodbye to David and the many new friends I had come to know, and stepped up into the train. The twenty hours on the train up to Bangkok were uneventful. The beautiful views from the windows of vast rice fields against a hilly green backdrop were familiar to me now. Even my overnight stay at the Bangkok mission house was pleasant and serene.

I flew to Hong Kong to meet up with two friends I'd met in Bible College. This was their hometown, and they toured me around the city, which included new dining adventures. I manoeu-

The King of Kings and I

vered my chopsticks to scrape out bits of seafood from their shells, and I experienced the flavours of chicken feet. Without access to the Thai curries and sweet rice, I lost five pounds that week.

I enjoyed the same wonderful hospitality I was given by my Thai hosts. My friends and their families graciously opened their homes to me, offering their best bed, their best room; the best of all they had. I said goodbye, knowing we would meet again in two weeks' time, back at Prairie.

On August 22nd I left Hong Kong at 7:00 in the evening to arrive in Oakland, California, at 8:20 that same evening. It felt satisfying to have gained back the time I lost when I first crossed the International Date Line.

The Oakland missionary guest house met all of the surrounding Californian neighbourhood standards. It was not a palace, but it was decadent. The entryway wrapped me up in its warmth of dark wood highlighted by rich reds and blues. A woman at the reception desk gave me information about the guest house and showed me up to my room. *Was the carpet really this plush? Had living two months on concrete floors only made it seem that my feet sank deep into such softness?*

After being shown to my room, I dropped my bags and looked around at all the furnishings—large bed, side tables, a chair, shelves, pictures, area rugs, lamps, drapes, and a closet. *Does a person really need all of this?* Soon I was asleep in the huge bed.

The next morning, I stared out my bedroom window. Short beige buildings stood compacted along pristine streets, and against a startling solid blue sky. So many shades of clean connected to the smooth and paved. Dirt and dust didn't seem to exist. But then neither did human beings since the streets were virtually empty. Just clean buildings on clean streets.

I walked down the stairs, tracing my hand along the dark wooden bannister and feeling every cushioned step. No line of ants traced itself anywhere on the walls or floors. In the quaint, quiet breakfast room I sat alone. I was back in North America, but it felt like another planet.

Before I went back upstairs, the woman at the reception desk stopped me with information regarding my airport arrangements. The return flight to Calgary wasn't until 4:00 p.m. so I was in no rush. Then she mentioned that the cost for my bed and breakfast stay was $50 American. I froze, my thoughts racing. *I didn't know I had to pay anything. Didn't OMF look after this? I don't have $50! What am I going to do?*

Still on a high travel alert and guarding all my valuables, I had taken my purse down to breakfast. Tucked away in my wallet I knew I had two Thai baht bills to keep as souvenirs. The 10 baht had its kingly equestrian statue, and the 20 baht showed a long boat with front pillars rising up into heads of sharp-toothed beasts like something from the book of Revelation. But I doubted that I had any significant amount of American money. As if performing on stage, I opened my purse to take out my wallet, because that is what people do when they are about to pay for something. *Why bother doing this? Do I even have any American money left? Why not just tell her?*

The King of Kings

Tax collectors asked Peter if Jesus, his teacher, pays the temple tax. Peter replied that he did. Then Jesus questioned Peter. "'What do you think, Simon?' he asked. 'From whom do the kings of the earth collect duty and taxes—from their own children or from others?' 'From others,' Peter answered" (Matthew 17:25b-26a).

Jesus pointed out the irony of the situation. He is Lord and King over everything, even the temple building. He was not required to pay any tax. Likewise Peter, since Peter belonged not only to the kingdom, but in following Christ, he was part of God's family.

Then Jesus said to Peter, "But so that we may not cause offense, go to the lake and throw out your line. Take the first fish you catch; open its mouth and you will find a four-drachma coin. Take it and give it to them for my tax and yours" (Matthew 17:27). And so a miracle happened. Out from the fish's mouth, Peter retrieved the exact amount. The taxes were paid and no one was offended. The tax collectors would neither understand the irony, nor see the miracle.

And I

I opened my wallet, wondering what amount of cash I might find. I saw three American bills—two twenties and a ten. I can't remember being so excited about paying a bill before. I think my hand shook when I handed her the exact amount.

God knew my need before I knew I had one. To me this was a miracle. I had spent American money in the airports and all the places where it was accepted, unaware of the need to hold back $50. But God ensured that I could pay my way home in full. Having exactly $50 showed me that God is precisely aware of our financial needs even if we are not. And as with Peter, God has the ability to meet them.

At the beginning of this journey, I prayed for $3,000 and I ended up paying everything in full to the last dollar. It gave me an odd sense of finality about my overseas adventure. The trip was completely paid for. No loose ends. It was over. I was back in North America with the distinct knowledge that God had taken care of me even in the smallest of details. I could trust Him for whatever lay ahead. Elisabeth Elliot says it well: "It is God to whom and with whom we travel, and while He is the end of the journey, He is also at every stopping place."

CHAPTER 29
The Box

In the mid-evening of August 23rd, I arrived back at the Calgary Airport where friends and family were waiting for me. It felt wonderful to be back home, hugging people who had supported me along the way. The timing worked well, because I had almost two weeks before the school year started. I needed that time to re-adjust.

As soon as I arrived in Calgary, I wondered where all the people were. The city felt empty as if a mass exodus had happened. Driving through residential areas required further processing. *Why do these people have spirit houses? No, wait a minute—those are bird houses.*

The days became busy. I took my film in to be developed, some into photographs and others into slides. I then prepared a presentation for my home church, bringing the congregation up to date with news about David and his ministries.

Because travelling to far-off places often affects the traveller, I began to notice a few changes in me. When not able to walk around two people chatting, I would pass between them, saying 'excuse me,' but now also with a little bow. At church or at a Bible study, I could no longer place my Bible directly on the floor beside me even if the floor had lovely carpet. Something like a notebook or my purse had to go in between. And I would place nothing on top of my Bible. Although no longer in the Buddhist culture where the upholding of honourable things mattered, some of these practices came home with me.

After time in the city and at my parents' home, I felt readjusted and ready for two more years of school. September arrived, and I was back sitting in desks, listening, taking notes, and occasionally

The King of Kings and I

looking out the windows at the prairie.

I soon became involved in a Laotian refugee ministry. About every three weeks, a team of us would drive from Three Hills into Calgary to help with a Laotian church's Sunday school. Our fellowship afterward, eating Asian food and chatting, often left me with the welcome sense that I was back in Thailand. One Sunday we stopped in Calgary's Chinatown before heading north to Three Hills. In the grocery store I spotted small boxes of durian cookies. Curiosity won over common sense and I bought one. Back at the college, in the absence of my roommate, I left the box of cookies on my desk. Later my roommate entered our dorm room and smelled an offensive odour. She left, but not until she had changed her socks, wondering if the problem was her. The cookies soon found their way to the garbage.

The new clothes I acquired in Thailand expanded my wardrobe, but once the colder weather hit, old sweaters covered up everything new. I thought about how nice it would be to have some new clothes to see me through the next two years of school. Two words came to mind when I thought about this desire—'selfish' and 'materialistic.' But then another word stood out—'powerless.' I couldn't actually do anything about this, because whatever money I could reasonably expect would have to go toward my tuition.

But I was not totally powerless. There was one thing I could do— I could pray. So I asked God for new clothes. In my prayer I made it clear—as if God needs clarification on anything—that I knew this was a want and not a need. I let God know that it would be fine if He did not give me any clothes. Having seen the poverty in Thailand, I knew I was extremely wealthy compared to most people in the world. I knew my request could not compare to the prayers of a refugee or a person suffering with leprosy.

The King of Kings

Why can't I just be content with what I have? "But godliness with contentment is great gain. For we brought nothing into the world, and we can take nothing out of it. But if we have food and clothing, we will be content with that" (1 Timothy 6:6-8). Why was contentment with my clothes so elusive for me? But I kept thinking how I was powerless, and how powerful God was.

In the same passage, Paul reminds Timothy of who God is. "God, the blessed and only Ruler, the King of kings and Lord of lords" (1 Timothy 6:15b).

This is the God I had become better acquainted with, the King of all kings. I now knew things about God from being in Thailand that I hadn't known before. He can do anything. He can bring light to my life in the darkness of Bangkok. He can ensure I have $50 when I need it. Nothing is too hard for God. He is the One we are encouraged to approach through his Son, Jesus Christ, our advocate.

"For we do not have a high priest who is unable to empathize with our weaknesses, but we have one who has been tempted in every way, just as we are—yet he did not sin. Let us then approach God's throne of grace with confidence, so that we may receive mercy and find grace to help us in our time of need" (Hebrews 4:15-16).

This was not a time of need. I didn't need clothes, but perhaps this was more about a need for something else—the need to take a step of faith and believe that God could do what He chose to do. Maybe I just wanted to let God know that I knew He could provide clothes for me. Whether He did or didn't was not the issue. Believing that God could do this was the issue.

"And without faith it is impossible to please God, because anyone who comes to him must believe that he exists and that he rewards those who earnestly seek him" (Hebrews 11:6).

And I

Five days later the weekend arrived, and I had arranged to go home to visit my parents. As soon as I entered the front door, my Mom told me about a conversation she had with the woman next door, whom I hardly knew. Her daughter-in-law had a huge box of clothes that she no longer wanted, and would I be interested in them?

Before I had prayed, or perhaps even while I prayed, a woman in another town was packing up a box of clothes, hoping someone could use them.

"Consider how the wild flowers grow. They do not labor or spin. Yet I tell you, not even Solomon in all his splendor was dressed like one of these. If that is how God clothes the grass of the field, which is here today, and tomorrow is thrown into the fire, how much more will he clothe you—you of little faith!" (Luke 12:27-28).

Receiving the box of clothes did not prompt me to start a prayer list for other things I wanted. It doesn't work that way with God. This answer to prayer became more than having new clothes. It showed me God's desire for relationship. He wants to delight in us. This needs to be made known. I didn't see my Mom's neighbour that weekend to thank her. But I wrote her a thank-you note. She needed to know that God worked through the kindness of her family. She needed to know that God is real.

"Faith does not operate in the realm of the possible. There is no glory for God in that which is humanly possible" (George Müller).

CHAPTER 30
Honesty

Sophomore and freshmen students concentrate on their studies. It is the junior and senior students who, while maintaining their studies, grow increasingly excited or panicky about their future. They will soon leave their comfortable routine environment. What will they do next? Planning needs to begin.

Even when I started at Prairie, I did not have a plan, or a desire, or even a clue about what I would do after my four years at Prairie. Having gone on a mission trip, I began to consider becoming an overseas missionary. Did I have a sense of being called to the mission field overseas? No, but then I didn't have a sense of being called to anything.

I allowed myself to feel pressured. Everyone else seemed to know what they'd be doing come the end of April 1985. I reasoned that the most logical plan for me was to become a full-time overseas missionary. Missionaries are sorely needed overseas. I did not have anything in Canada to hold me back and was completely free to spend the rest of my life anywhere doing mission work. Yes, that must be the way to go.

OMF was an obvious choice because of my experience with them. They knew me, and I liked the mission. I talked this over with my parents, and although they didn't like the idea of me living overseas so far from home, they wanted me to make my own decisions, to do what I wanted to do.

I proceeded with an application with OMF to become a full time missionary upon completion of my senior year. I allowed my availability to remain open to working in any Southeast Asian country that OMF served. My aptitude test showed that I shouldn't have any problem learning another language. Soon OMF even had a copy of my dental records. Everything was set for the end of April, after graduation, when as a missionary candidate I would begin raising support money.

As I went further into my senior year of studies, having been approved by OMF, I plodded along class after class, week by week. The word 'plodding' in the *Oxford Canadian Dictionary* means "to walk doggedly, or laboriously, to trudge."

I trudged.

One day while I was standing in the cafeteria line, two girls ahead of me were excitedly discussing their future. The bitter voice in my heart surprised me. *You guys are so lucky to be able to do what you want.* I kept trudging laboriously around the campus but felt increasingly against the idea of going overseas. But what else would I do? God *must* want me to be a missionary.

Joyless weeks continued. Several rules at school had changed so that, at breakfast, the men and women could sit together. I sat at my usual table chatting with my usual friends over our usual two cups of coffee. One friend expressed concern for me because he noticed how depressed I was getting. Later, he questioned whether God was really calling me to the mission field overseas. He knew I loved to travel, so he suggested that I stay in Canada and work for a travel agency. I laughed. *How terribly absurd and secular. How could something like that be what God wanted me to do?* Wait a minute—was I detecting pride in myself? As if, other people (e.g. travel agents) may not have a high spiritual calling, but I do. *God must want me to be a missionary, doesn't He?*

That night with my roommate away for the weekend, I sat on my bed, deeply depressed. I had been depressed for well over six months. Something had to change. "A wish changes nothing – a decision changes everything" (Anonymous).

After almost five years of walking with God, I should have known that I didn't have to be afraid to come to Him in total honesty. But I was afraid. I had asked for clothes and money without being afraid. But now I was about to be honest about something that I was sure would disappoint God, maybe even make Him angry. But I had to be honest.

At first I said to God that I didn't want to go overseas as a missionary. Then I decided to say what I really wanted to say, "God, I am not going to go overseas."

There—I said it.

I wasn't carrying a physical burden on my shoulders, but I might as well have been, because just then a massive weight fell off me. I was free.

The King of Kings

"Kings take pleasure in honest lips; they value the one who speaks what is right" (Proverbs 16:13).

Our omniscient God knows our attitudes, feelings, motives, and thoughts. He understands everything about us. There is nothing we can hide from him. Patiently He waited for me to arrive at a place in my life where I would approach Him in honesty.

There was no need for me to justify my feelings or my depression. The only thing I said to God was a tearful 'thank you.' "Come to me, all you who are weary and burdened, and I will give you rest. Take my yoke upon you and learn from me, for I am gentle and humble in heart, and you will find rest for your souls. For my yoke is easy and my burden is light" (Matthew 11:28-30).

I did not have God's peace until I was honest. Circumstances in my life had lined up straighter than a ruler showing me that an overseas career was a wide-open door. But that door needed to be even wider. God wanted me to be available for a life of missions anywhere. It took me a long time to realize that within what I thought were the perfect circumstances, the peace and joy of the Holy Spirit were absent. Peace and joy are important. "May the God of hope fill you with all joy and peace as you trust in him, so that you may overflow with hope by the power of the Holy Spirit" (Romans 15:13).

And I

Friends at Prairie, and even some teachers, noticed an immediate difference in me, as if I had become a different person. I like to think it was me going back to being the person God intended me to be. I was myself. I was at peace. My uncertain future had me excited. All the world was opened wide to me now. The excitement in my voice was obvious when I would say to friends, "I don't know what I will be doing after graduation!"

It is not always easy to undo what we have done. I contacted OMF and began to straighten things out, knowing that I had disappointed the mission board, and yet they understood. "Many are the plans in a person's heart, but it is the Lord's purpose that prevails" (Proverbs 19:21). To not have a plan was better than having a plan that was not from God.

CHAPTER 31
Walk in Wisdom

On April 21, 1985 I graduated from Prairie Bible Institute, receiving a Bachelor of Religious Education degree (B.R.E.) along with an Evangelical Teacher Training Association diploma (E.T.T.A.). Paul Maxwell, President of Prairie, son of L.E. Maxwell the co-founder of the college, handed out our degrees and diplomas and gave the benediction.

Our graduating class had the privilege of having Elisabeth Elliot as our guest speaker. Although Elisabeth Elliot had re-married, it is the story of her first husband that the world knows best. Jim and Elisabeth Elliot served as missionaries in Ecuador. In seeking to reach the native group called the Aucas, Jim and four other men died in a spear attack by members of the Quichua tribe. This became world news, and a U.S. search team was sent to retrieve the five bodies from the beach where the men had been killed. Despite this horrendous loss, the sacrifices of these men led the mission to achieve the goals for God's kingdom, impacting thousands around the world. Elisabeth Elliot stayed to live and minister among the Quichua tribe, learning their language and raising her and Jim's baby daughter among them.

In her book, *Discipline: The Glad Surrender*, Elisabeth Elliot wrote: "I never appreciated the therapeutic value of work until I lost my first husband. Since then I have been asked dozens of times, 'How did you ever bring yourself to go back to the jungle?' I doubt that I could have. I did not 'go back.' I stayed. There was work to be done, lots of work."

Elisabeth Elliot delivered an inspiring challenge, related to our graduating theme, 'Walk in Wisdom.' "The fear of the Lord is the beginning of wisdom; all who follow his precepts have good understanding. To him belongs eternal praise" (Psalm 111:10).

I was leaving behind four years of excellent teaching and incredible experiences. I was leaving the college, knowing the Word of God better, and realizing that my study of the Scriptures had only just begun. One thing about spending four years studying the Word of God, you come away realizing how little you actually know of the inexhaustible Scriptures.

After the graduating class sang a song, which I was not exempt from, we stepped outside the tabernacle into the blizzard-like conditions. Across the campus in the dining room, refreshments had been prepared, providing a place to socialize with family and friends.

The great exchange of yearbooks, to capture friends' written blessings, continued right up to the last minutes of graduation day. I said goodbye to the many friends I had made over the four years and packed my few belongings into my parent's car. After dinner out with my family, I stayed with my parents a few days and then headed to Calgary, where God had plans for me.

About a month before graduation, my friend Carolyn shared news of a job opportunity with a small oil and gas company. From Three Hills I had a telephone interview with the president of the company. He asked about my experience with computers. I had none. I couldn't even properly visualize a computer. I thought it must be a huge machine taking up half an office. What I did have was a willingness to learn, and that was good enough for him. At the end of the conversation, this Christian man hired me.

I found this new, but somehow familiar, direction in my life exciting. I would be back working in an office, doing what I loved to do. It wouldn't be an easy door to walk through, since a new job always comes with challenges, but this direction also came with God's peace. It would be with God's peace that I would step into the newness of the computer world, new people to get to know, and a new time in my life.

"Commit to the Lord whatever you do, and he will establish your plans. The Lord works out everything to its proper end" (Proverbs 16:3-4a).

The King of Kings and I

The King of Kings

Valuable lessons can be learned from every king who ruled over Judah and Israel, and from every king or queen who rules today. We see their influence upon each of their kingdoms. Their examples can teach us both what to do and what not to do.

Once David was established as king, his reign became marked by a steadfastness to follow God. Like all the kings that ruled over Judah and Israel, David was fallible, but despite his sins, he continued to pursue God's heart. He knew the kingdom he ruled over was nothing compared to God's kingdom.

David expressed the importance of God's kingdom in many of his psalms. "All your works praise you, Lord; your faithful people extol you. They tell of the glory of your kingdom and speak of your might, so that all people may know of your mighty acts and the glorious splendor of your kingdom. Your kingdom is an everlasting kingdom, and your dominion endures through all generations" (Psalm 145:10-13a).

During my four years at college, I saw Christ as a powerful King. One who rules with compassion and understanding. Now back in Calgary, I wanted to continue my pursuit of this glorious King of kings, in the manner of King David. I love Prairie's motto, "To know Christ and make Him known," and I carried that with me back to Calgary. I had learned through my studies and my experiences that God wants us to be missionaries wherever we are. The *Oxford Canadian Dictionary* defines 'mission' as "a particular task or goal assigned to a person or group of people" and the word 'missionary' as "concerned with or characteristic of religious mission". The words 'heat', 'humidity', 'overseas', and 'jungle' are conspicuously missing.

Walking in wisdom means to accept God's assignment for me. It is about doing God's mission and not stumbling along with my own plans. Sometimes the plan of our lives is not always clear at first. If our true desire is to follow Christ, then Christ will enable us to follow Him and not get lost. As we continue walking with God, discovering His plan, it becomes God Himself that we discover.

A man that Jesus healed subsequently wanted to follow Christ. But his idea of how to do that differed from Christ's plan. "As Jesus was getting into the boat, the man who had been demon-possessed begged to go with him. Jesus did not let him, but said, 'Go home to your own people and tell them how much the Lord has done for you, and how he has had mercy on you.' So the man went away and began to tell in the Decapolis how much Jesus had done for him. And all the people were amazed" (Mark 5:18-20).

Christ's plan for him did not include getting into the boat with the disciples and crossing waters to new lands. This man had a profound story of Christ and His kingdom to tell. And the best place for him to do that was in his home territory of Decapolis. By doing this, he was following Christ's mission.

And I

For me, it took a while to transition from small town college life to the city life I once knew so well. Returning to Calgary was not going to be like stepping back into a comfortable pair of shoes. The economy had recovered but not to the extent it once was. The downtown core had grown. Historic old buildings had been torn down and replaced with taller ones. I found myself in a jungle of grey concrete, getting lost in a place that I used to know so well.

Because rules no longer surrounded me, I had to make my own life-style choices. After work I wandered through the department stores and boutiques in search of affordable business clothes. The mid-eighties' fashions were frightening. Everything was big and colourful. Big hair, giant earrings, massive shoulder pads, saucer-size buttons, and a hundred and one ways to wrap a loud silk scarf around your neck. I began to see my Bible college days as a simpler, gentler time when clothes came in a neighbour's box, and rules gave me guidance.

When I first moved back to Calgary to search for an apartment, I stayed with a church elder and his wife. After church one day, I asked if they thought it ok for me to put in a load of laundry. For my four college years, Sundays were pleasant days of rest, where I didn't do laundry, homework, or any kind of study. The church elder didn't tell me what to do. All he said was, "Well, Kim, what I do know is that if you wash your clothes today, you will end up with clean clothes." Since that was what I wanted, I put in a load.

This freedom called for me to make choices that took prayerful thought. It was up to me now to decide. Is this skirt too short? Are blue jeans appropriate? Is it ok to do laundry on Sundays? I felt like a teenager trying to discover who I was.

I got involved in church ministries involving teaching and outreach. I attended prayer groups. My life was enriched because of my knowing more about the Bible, having insights about the world we are in, and personally knowing God better. Gradually life seemed to be settling. But it seems that in God's plan, life never stays settled for very long.

Only a few months after my graduation, I would need to lean heavily on my past experiences with God. I would need to keep trusting in His love for me when my dad suddenly died and my world became very dark. That same year I would need to count on God's guidance when one Sunday in the sanctuary I noticed a man called Ian, and his then nine-year-old son Jeremy, and my world became very bright. Brighter still when three years later we would marry and become a family. Here Elisabeth Elliot's words proved true again: "God will never disappoint us. He loves us and has only one purpose for us—holiness, which in His kingdom equals joy."

***

I pray for you morning & night, especially that you keep well and able to adjust to so many changes. I know God is with you. Love Mom & Dad

Mom & Dad, Thank you for your prayers. God has been very faithful to me.

Notes

CHANGE
- https://www.goodreads.com/quotes/20149-nothing-happens-until-something-moves
- https://www.goodreads.com/quotes/7022252-do-not-ask-god-to-guide-your-footsteps-if-you-re

Chapter 1
- http://www.cbc.ca/history/EPISCONTENTSE1EP17CH-3PA1LE.html

Chapter 2
- Mark Hanson, "His Ways are Higher." *The Prairian 1982 Yearbook*, Volume 31, Prairie Bible Institute, Three Hills, AB
- James Strong, *The New Strong's Exhaustive Concordance of the Bible* (Nashville, Tennessee: Thomas Nelson Publishers, 1984) Hebrew word #3519

Chapter 3
- https://www.brainyquote.com/authors/oliver_wendell_holmes_jr
- *New Strong's*, Greek word #4163

Chapter 4
- https://home.snu.edu/~hculbert/slogans.htm
- https://omf.org/ca/about-omf/our-story/cim-omf/

Chapter 5
- https://www.christianquotes.info/quotes-by-author/hudson-taylor-quotes/#axzz57KwC9Nhf
- Map; Overseas Missionary Fellowship, 1983

TRAVEL
- http://gretastravels.com/20-best-travel-quotes/
- https://www.shmoop.com/quotes/were-not-in-kansas-anymore.html

Chapter 6
- http://recycling.about.com/od/Resources/fl/How-Long-Does-It-Take-Garbage-to-Decompose.htm
- Norman L. Geisler and William E. Nix, *A General Introduction to the Bible* (Moody Press, Chicago 1968 p 227-228)

Chapter 7
- C.S. Lewis, *Surprised by Joy* (Williams Collins Sons & Co. Ltd. Glasgow 1955, p 127)
- http://www.travelandleisure.com/articles/singapore-girl-flying-college
- http://www.dailymail.co.uk/travel/travel_news/article-2932968/World-s-outrageous-flight-attendant-uniforms.html
- https://www.goodreads.com/author/quotes/5825213.George_Muller

Chapter 8
- https://www.britannica.com/place/Dead-Sea

Chapter 10
- https://www.smithsonianmag.com/science-nature/why-does-the-durian-fruit-smell-so-terrible 149205532/
- https://www.healthline.com/nutrition/durian-fruit
- https://en.wikipedia.org/wiki/The_King_and_I
- http://womenshistory.about.com/od/leonowensanna/a/anna_king_true.htm
- http://members.tripod.com/king_anna/leonowens.html
- https://quotes.thefamouspeople.com/george-muller-3815.php

BEGIN
- https://twitter.com/davewillis/status/782932579167199232
- https://brightdrops.com/dr-seuss-quotes

Chapter 11
- Information Sheet: OMF – Christian Hospital, Saiburi, Pattani, South Thailand, 1983
- http://www.bamboobotanicals.ca/

- https://biblicaljoy.wordpress.com/2013/09/16/i-thessalonians-516-18-rejoice-pray-give-thanks/
- *New Strong's,* Hebrew word #3885

Chapter 12
- Information Sheet: OMF – Christian Hospital, Saiburi, Pattani, South Thailand, 1983
- https://www.who.int/lep/disease/en
- http://www.who.int/mediacentre/factsheets/fs101/en/
- https://omf.org/thailand/omf-thailand-history/
- *New Strong's,* Greek word #1651

Chapter 13
- https://www.kids-world-travel-guide.com/pacific-ocean-facts.html
- *New Strong's,* Hebrew word #4390
- https://www.biblestudytools.com/dictionary/divination/
- *Oxford Canadian Dictionary,* Oxford University Press (Don Mills Ontario, 2004).
- https://blog.logos.com/2015/06/in-memory-of-elisabeth-elliot-30-of-her-most-inspiring-quotes/

Chapter 14
- https://omf.org/thailand/omf-thailand-history/
- http://www.cbc.ca/archives/topic/boat-people-a-refugee-crisis
- http://www.cbc.ca/news/canada/calgary/vietnamese-boat-people-syrian-refugees-fundraiser-1.3350655
- https://en.wikipedia.org/wiki/Bhumibol_Adulyadej
- https://verticallivingministries.com/tag/minka-hanskamp/
- https://www.brainyquote.com/authors/jim_elliot

Chapter 15
- http://www.pattayaunlimited.com/huntsman-spider/
- https://www.thailandsnakes.com/thailand-snake-notes/most-common-snakes/

OBSERVE
- https://www.brainyquote.com/authors/robert_badenpowell
- https://ftw.usatoday.com/2015/09/the-50-greatest-yogi-berra-quotes

Chapter 16
- http://www.buddhist-temples.com/buddhism-facts/
- http://joythay.weebly.com/thai-superstitions.html
- http://www.thaibuddhism.net/principles.htm
- http://dabuddhabudda.weebly.com/worship-rituals-and-practices.html
- https://thebuddhistcentre.com/text/who-was-buddha
- *New Strong's*, Greek word #318, Greek word # 2431

Chapter 17
- http://www.ayutthaya-history.com/Temples_Ruins_Phanan-Choeng.html
- http://cavinglizsea.blogspot.ca/2011/12/wat-khuha-phimuk-yala-thailand.html
- http://www.lotussculpture.com/mudras.html
- http://www.thebuddhagarden.com/buddha-poses.html
- https://www.thaizer.com/thailand-photos/colours-of-thailand-gold/
- https://slumberpartyhostels.com/gold-in-buddhism-significance/
- *New Strong's*, Greek word #5461

Chapter 18
- http://www.islamicfoundation.ca/ramadan.aspx
- https://www.thoughtco.com/what-is-ramadan-2004619
- https://www.britannica.com/place/Malaysia/Religion
- https://www.timeanddate.com/holidays/muslim/ramadan-begins
- Information Sheet; Overseas Missionary Fellowship, 1983
- https://www.thoughtco.com/halal-eating-and-drinking-2004241
- *New Strong's*, Greek word #1657
- https://quotes.thefamouspeople.com/george-muller-3815.php

Chapter 19
- Map: Overseas Missionary Fellowship, 1983
- *New Strong's*, Greek word #3907

STRUGGLE
- https://www.azquotes.com/author/7843-Helen_Keller/tag/struggle
- https://keithcraft.org/grow-through-what-you-go-through

Chapter 21
- https://www.psalty.com/track/687833/in-his-time?feature_

id=140390 ("In His Time," words & music by Diane Ball 1978 Maranatha! Music CCLI No.25981)
- https://www.thespruce.com/how-to-make-kaya-coconut-jam-3217516
- https://www.thespruce.com/cooking-with-pandan-3217067
- http://www.biblestudy.org/question/why-did-king-david-wait-to-rule-israel.html
- https://www.neverthirsty.org/bible-qa/qa-archives/question/how-old-was-david-when-samuel-anointed-him-king/

Chapter 22
- http://www.thaitable.com/thai/recipe/black-beans-in-coconut-milk
- https://www.timeanddate.com/sun/thailand/Bangkok
- https://www.sunrise-and-sunset.com/en/sun/canada/calgary

Chapter 23
- http://learnthaiwithmod.com/2013/11/thai-national-anthem-%E0
- *New Strong's,* Greek word #220, Hebrew word #7368
- https://blog.logos.com/2015/06/in-memory-of-elisabeth-elliot-30-of-her-most-inspiring-quotes/

CONTRIBUTE
- https://www.brainyquote.com/quotes/john_c_maxwell_600909
- https://www.brainyquote.com/authors/winston_churchill

Chapter 25
- https://quotes.thefamouspeople.com/george-muller-3815.php

Chapter 26
- http://thaifoodandtravel.com/blog/the-mortar-and-pestle/

Chapter 27
- *New Strong's,* Hebrew word #7200
- https://www.goodreads.com/author/quotes/4693730.James_Hudson_Taylor

RETURN
- https://www.brainyquote.com/authors/nelson_mandela
- https://www.google.com/search?q=ibn+battuta+quotes

Chapter 28
- http://exploreforayear.com/inspiration/55-quotes-travel
- https://www.goodreads.com/quotes/301852-it-god-to-whom-and-with-whom-we-travel

Chapter 29
- https://quotes.thefamouspeople.com/george-muller-3815.php

Chapter 30
- *Oxford Canadian Dictionary*
- https://twitter.com/hvmn/status/676930267550978049

Chapter 31
- http://www.christianity.com/church/church-history/church-history-for-kids/jim-elliot-no-fool-11634862.html
- https://www.thegospelcoalition.org/article/9-things-you-should-know-about-elisabeth-elliot
- Elisabeth Elliot, *Discipline: The Glad Surrender*, (Fleming H. Revell, 1982, p. 131)
- *Oxford Canadian Dictionary*

www.ingramcontent.com/pod-product-compliance
Lightning Source LLC
Chambersburg PA
CBHW071245070526
44583CB00017B/2336